MW01519070

FAITH AMID THE COVID-19 CRISIS

The effect of pandemics on the Church and Christian faith

To: Sister Dell
"With God, all things are possible!"
2023-10-23

CLAUDETTE E. MILLER

Copyright © 2023

All rights reserved. No part of this book may be reproduced or transmitted
in any form or by any means without written permission of the publisher, except in the case of brief quotations embedded in critical articles
and reviews.

Statements made and opinions expressed in this publication are those of the
author and do not necessarily reflect the views of the publisher or indicate
an endorsement by the publisher.

ISBN: 978-1-948777-41-4

Dedication

I dedicate this book to three incredible women: my late mother, Gloria Lacey; my late great-grand-aunt, Alva Lacey; and my late Sunday school teacher, Evangelist Nembhard. These individuals were towers of strength who laid foundations for me to succeed. Their influence in my life inspired my motto: Salvation + Education = Success!

My mother instilled the value of education in me from a young age. To her, I ascribe this verse of scripture, "Study to shew thyself approved unto God, a workman that needeth not to be ashamed, rightly dividing the word of truth" (2 Tim. 2:15).

To my great-grand-aunt, who was the embodiment of the Proverbs 31 woman (vv. 10-31), I attribute this passage of scripture, "Train up a child in the way he should go: And when he is old, he will not depart from it" (Prov. 22:6).

A testament to the proverb, "It takes a village to raise a child," Evangelist Nembhard encouraged me to learn my Sunday School lessons thoroughly so that I was prepared to recite them when called upon. This helped develop my confidence in public speaking. She exemplifies this passage of scripture, "when I call to remembrance the unfeigned faith that is in thee, which dwelt first in thy grandmother Lois, and thy mother Eunice; and I am persuaded that in thee also" (2 Tim. 1:5).

Acknowledgments

Dr. Michael M.C. Reardon; Academic Dean/Professor
Thank you for identifying the distinct potential of a book coming from my thesis. Quietly, I embarked on the journey.

Denise Grant; International Bestselling Author of *Racism: Rising Above the Discomfort of Difficult Conversations*
Thank you for sharing your insights into the journey of authoring a book, which you completed recently.

My father, siblings, other family members, friends, and colleagues.
Thank you for your support and your encouragement. When you did not hear from me, I was saturated with completing this project.

Bishop Dr. Audley N. James (1937 - 2019); Founder/Sr. Pastor, Revival Time Tabernacle Worldwide Ministries
I commenced studies in theology based on a calling from God, first identified several years before by the late Bishop. His wisdom and encouragement resonated with me to pursue the calling that is affording me new opportunities, such as preaching the gospel and authoring a book.

Thank you to everyone on the editing team who helped to make this book come alive—I love the book cover design. A special thanks to my publisher—Mwale and Chantel Henry of the Bestsellers Academy—you were truly a great source of inspiration to me in bringing this book to fruition.

Foreword

As an academic dean and professor, I am often approached by students who have a "book idea" or want to turn their master's thesis or doctoral dissertation into a publication. While I am more than happy to assist them in their endeavors, few of these dreams ultimately materialize, often due to pastoral or familial responsibilities. With Claudette, the situation was entirely different. Due to being her supervisor, I was the first person to read her thesis. I immediately recognized that her project filled a lacuna within examinations of fostering or sustaining ecclesial health. Specifically, I was impressed with her integration of history, theology, and quantitative research to clearly articulate the significant and irreplaceable role of in-person church gatherings in Christian discipleship. And thus, it is with great joy that I commend the ensuing volume to you, the reader.

Christianity in the twenty-first century may be characterized as variegated streams of theology, praxis, ethnic, and denominational orientations. Yet, a significant issue unifying many of these otherwise divergent traditions is a turn toward the digital world—whether *via* television, streaming services, or Zoom meetings. Thus, the COVID-19 pandemic, I suggest, did not give rise to a new model of (the) church then, but rather, accelerated this pre-existing shift to virtual gatherings. This of course is a controversial statement, and countless church leaders spanning the denominational spectrum argue otherwise. It was the pandemic, they boldly assert, that pushed them into hybrid meetings. And now with their congregants comfortable attending Lord's Day meetings in their pajamas, *who are they to ask them to stop?* The gospel is still the gospel whether proclaimed in-person or delivered by combinations of bits and bytes, they suggest, and not forsaking "assembling together" (Heb. 10:25) can be fulfilled by seeing digital faces on variously sized monitors.

For Claudette, such statements were worthy of investigation. Her opening chapters carefully trace historic pandemics from the first century onward, and thereafter, detail how the Church universally responded to these challenges. Narrowing her focus in chapters 3-5, Claudette discusses and analyzes the results of surveys she distributed to congregations in the Greater Toronto area. In doing so, she discovered a surprising (at least to some) result: there is a tangible difference between in-person and virtual gatherings; Christians, broadly speaking, *do desire in-person gatherings*; and perhaps, the health of congregations is, at least partially, dependent upon real, authentic face-to-face fellowship and interactions.

Based upon these results, Claudette outlines challenges, changes, and recommendations for the post-pandemic Church in chapters 6 and 7. In these particularly illuminating chapters, she suggests that pastors cannot simply return to their pre-pandemic practices, but must incorporate both in-person and virtual components into their services. To be sure, God is sovereign, even over the devices and schemes of the enemy. While in-person gatherings engender greater ecclesial health, there nevertheless remains a role for technology in the twenty-first-century church. An international reach of the gospel, maintaining some level of fellowship with anxious congregants, and allowing elderly or disabled individuals to be cared for are all valid reasons for pastors not merely to return to their old ways. And thus, the sovereignty of God over even the most unfortunate of circumstances necessitates a reimagining of what (the) church can and should be.

In the final three chapters of her book, Claudette turns from analysis to synthesis: *what does this all mean—for the church, for the faith, and for you?* These chapters represent, perhaps, the most spiritually edifying aspects of Claudette's ambitious endeavor. Can disease, fear, anxiety, and governmental involvement quench the life of the Church? Should afflictions, depression, or mistreatment cause one's faith to falter? In the face of negative circumstances, how should a God-fearing and God-loving person respond? Claudette's answers to these questions are well worth your time and thoughtful reflection.

The implications of Claudette's examination of the Church, the faith, and the individual Christian when faced with adversity are manifold. As Christians, we are *in the world,* and thus, must live in a prudent way, exercising caution and remaining safe for the preservation of life—even if only to have more time on this earth to preach the good news. On the other hand, we are not *of the world.* We possess a faith that overcomes the world (1 John 5:4), a peace which surpasses all understanding (Phil. 4:7), and a hope of our calling that extends beyond this world into the next (Eph. 1:18). In the midst of adversity, we are called to be shining lights to the world, proclaiming the fullness of God's economy to all those we meet. This is what it means to be a member of the Body of Christ in a post-pandemic world. Ultimately, *this* should be (and indeed, must be) "the effect of pandemics on the Church and Christian faith."

-*Dr. Michael M.C. Reardon; Academic Dean, Canada Christian College and School of Graduate Theological Studies*

Reader Testimonials

What others are saying about *Faith Amid the COVID-19 Crisis - The effect of pandemics on the Church and Christian faith:*

"Infused with illuminating ideas and gripping historical insight, Claudette Miller captures the reader's attention. In a post-pandemic world, we are challenged and left with the words of the master, "Let your light so shine before men, that they may see your good works, and glorify your Father which is in heaven."
— **Dr. Andrew James, Professor/Pastor**

"As faith leaders have adapted and prayerfully sought to flourish in the aftermath of Covid, Claudette has courageously and boldly asked the "how" and "why" questions in order to provide clarity on the effects of the pandemic on the Church and Christian Faith. Claudette has in effect helped articulate an understanding and created a collaborative picture for church leaders who are looking for answers and solutions to their next steps. A must-read for all clergy and spiritual leaders!"
— **Rev. Andrea Christensen | Rector**

"This book is an interesting, insightful, and instructive read–
it challenges the reader to self-assessment with respect to the
impact COVID-19 has had on the Christian faith/church.
Claudette Miller seeks to reinforce the foundation on which
followers of Christ must stand while keeping the return of Jesus
top of mind. Personal stories and testimonials are shared as well
as exhortations to encourage Believers in Christ to persevere in
the things of God and to trust the sovereignty of God amidst
adversity. I was impressed with the quality and depth of data
presented in the research including interviews with faith leaders and people within the Church community. Although the
Church, leaders, and believers faced many challenges during
the pandemic, there were also many victories, acts of kindness,
sacrifice, and generosity. This book will provoke you to think
about your faith, leaving you to ask questions about the future
and restoring your hope that in the midst of darkness there is
a light that shines through."

— **Rev. Dr. Tony Soldano, Dean, Executive Leadership
Institute, Canada Christian College**

Preface

"The wealthiest place in the world is not the gold mines of South America or the oil fields of Iraq or Iran. They are not the diamond mines of South Africa or the banks of the world. The wealthiest place on the planet is just down the road. It is the cemetery. There lie buried companies that were never started, inventions that were never made, bestselling books that were never written, and masterpieces that were never painted. In the cemetery is buried the greatest treasure of untapped potential."

— Dr. Myles Munroe

This book was written out of an intrinsic desire to share what I learned about the COVID-19 pandemic and the Church while writing my thesis for my Master of Divinity at Canada Christian College & School of Graduate Theological Studies. The findings are based on empirical research in which I undertook a qualitative study that consisted of conducting interviews with seven church leaders and administering an online questionnaire to 100 volunteer congregants, from seven different denominations in the Greater Toronto Area (GTA).

My thesis topic, *The Effects of the COVID-19 Pandemic on the Church and Its Affiliates and The Response of the Church to the Pandemic,* revealed that most respondents prefer in-person church over virtual (online) church.

The outcome of my research concluded the COVID-19 pandemic did not weaken the desire of churchgoers to continue to assemble as the Scriptures command, "not forsaking the assembling of ourselves together…" (Heb. 10:25). The Church did not give up due to the order of the government to close the Church. Instead, the Church employed other means to meet. I also discovered that the Church would continue to remain relevant, and its perseverance is best encapsulated in this refrain:

"Let the Church be the Church;

Let the People rejoice.

Oh, we've settled the question;

We've made our choice.

Let the anthems ring out,

Songs of victory swell;

For the Church triumphant is alive and well" *(Gaither, 1973).*

Table of Contents

List of Tables

Introduction

Have you ever had an experience that left you feeling helpless, full of doubts and searching for answers that you felt would never come? Often, we find ourselves in these situations wondering, "How am I possibly going to get through this?", "Who is going to help me?", "Will God help me?" The COVID-19 pandemic has brought up some similar questions and worries for many of us, as we saw people riddled with fear, societies filled with disruptiveness, and countless lives lost.

This pandemic was often referred to as "uncharted territory;" however, pandemics are not a new phenomenon. This was not the first time the world has encountered something like this, and it might not be the last. A "pandemic" is defined as "an outbreak of a disease that occurs over a wide geographic area (such as multiple countries or continents) and typically affects a significant proportion of the population" (Merriam-Webster, 2022).

We will start by looking at multiple pandemics that occurred in the past, comparing their effects with those of COVID-19. When considering this virus and the impact it has had on our world, the Church specifically, we first need to examine the response of the Church to previous pandemics. This will give us helpful information, as we look forward to what it means for the future of the Church. COVID-19 shook up the world. It made some people question their faith, and it helped others find or strengthen theirs. We will dig deep into the specific effects that COVID-19 had on the Church, and the difference that it should make for us as believers as we continue to live out our Christian faith. We will examine what the effects of COVID-19 mean in our own lives and why it should cause us to prepare for the end times, not out of fear and trepidation, but out of the hope and anticipation of Heaven.

Before we dive in, let's examine what the Bible has to say about pandemics through Scriptural deduction. In Luke, it says:

"... and there will be great earthquakes in various places, and famines and pestilences; and there will be fearful sights and great signs from heaven" (Luke 21:11). The term "Pestilence" is a synonym for pandemics. It refers to "any sudden fatal epidemic."

It derives from the Latin word, "pestis," meaning "plague" (Bible Study Tools, 2022). While pandemics may be "unprecedented" to us, they are no surprise to God. He remains in control no matter the circumstances we face.

Chapter One:
Pandemics Throughout History

We can learn a lot from history. When we look back at our world history, cultural history, our heritage, or our personal history, it can give us insight moving forward. We may see positive examples in the past that we can follow. We may see mistakes made that we need to avoid repeating. In our own lives and the lives of those we love, we can look back and see how God has provided, and trust that He will continue to do so. Our history may be part of us, but it does not define us. For me personally, when I look back at my own life, I am reminded of these truths: even when I struggle, God's grace abounds; even when things look a lot different than what I would have planned, God is right beside me leading the way; even when things feel hopeless, God provides a way. There have been times in my life I have felt lonely, but I have never been left alone. There have been moments of uncertainty, but God has remained steadfast.

COVID-19 brought about something most of us had never experienced, and it became difficult, even in the lives of Christians, to hold on to hope. It became hard to see anything past what was right in front of our eyes. COVID-19 was especially agonizing for the Church, as it was forced to close its doors for the first time in over 100 years. This lockdown had major impacts on the leaders and congregants within the Church.

While COVID-19 felt new and scary to many of us, history is filled with pandemics and people just like us wondering what in the world is happening. To properly assess the impact of COVID-19, we first need to take a closer look at the pandemics over the years that are considered to have "changed history" (Editors, 2021, December 21). Though COVID-19 was, by far, the most impactful one many of us have experienced in our lifetime, there have been numerous pandemics over the centuries. SARS, being the most recent, comes to mind.

Leprosy

One of the earliest recorded pandemics is actually found in the Bible. It's called leprosy and is referenced on several occasions. For example, 2 Chronicles 26:20-23 talks about King Uzziah who had leprosy. 2 Kings 5:1 and 5:27 both refer to a soldier who had leprosy. Matthew 8:3, Mark 1:40-42, and Luke 5:13 all describe the moment when Jesus healed a man of leprosy. Then, in Luke 17:11-19, the story of the ten lepers whom Jesus healed is documented. "Leprosy," with various connotations, is mentioned, "55 times in the Old Testament (Hebrew = *tsara'ath*) and 13 times in the New Testament (Greek = *lepros, lepra*)" (Gillen, 2009, October 25).

During Bible days, leprosy was seen as punishment from God for sin. It was reported as a pandemic of the 11th Century during the Middle Ages in Europe, which resulted in numerous leprosy-focused hospitals being built to accommodate the enormous number of victims (Editors, 2021, December 21).

Another early pandemic occurred in Athens in 430 B.C., (of the same name) during the Peloponnesian War between Athens and Sparta, the two most powerful cities in ancient Greece at that time. It is said that after the disease passed through Libya, Ethiopia, and Egypt, it crossed over into Greece and killed approximately two-thirds of the population (Editors, 2021, December 21). Can you imagine ⅔ of the population being wiped out by a disease? That's 67% of your friends, your neighbourhood and your family members. I can't fathom witnessing something like this and having the strength to move forward.

ANTONINE PLAGUE

The Antonine Plague of 165 A.D. is also considered one of the original pandemics. This could have been an early appearance of smallpox that began with the Huns. It is believed that the Huns infected the Germans, who in turn infected the Romans. After this, the disease spread throughout the Roman Empire and continued until about 180 A.D. (Editors, 2021, December 21).

CYPRIAN PLAGUE

In 250 A.D., the next early pandemic, the Cyprian Plague, emerged. This pandemic was named after Thascius Caecilius Cyprianus, Bishop of Cartage, who ended up dying from it (Editors, 2021, December 21). This plague lasted nearly 20 years and during its peak, killed as many as 5,000 people a day. Needless to say, it took a toll on the Roman world, exhausting the population and causing inner turmoil in those who thought the world was ending (World History Encyclopedia, 2022).

Justinian Plague

The Justinian Plague of 541 A.D followed the Cyprian Plague. It is believed to have been the first significant appearance of the bubonic plague. This plague began in Egypt and then spread through Palestine, the Byzantine Empire, and throughout the Mediterranean (Editors, 2021, December 21). History records this as an impactful pandemic "with recurrences over the next two centuries resulting in the deaths of approximately 50 million people." At that time, this was noted as "constituting 26 per cent of the world population" (Editors, 2021, December 21). We think COVID-19 has lasted a long time, being prevalent for a couple of years… this plague continued to infect people for around 200 years! Another interesting fact about this pandemic is that it squashed Emperor Justinian's (reign 527–565) plans to resurrect the Roman Empire. It sparked enormous economic upheaval and created an apocalyptic atmosphere that prompted the rapid spread of Christianity (Editors, 2021, December 21). Many questioned if this was the end of the world and sought out hope in Jesus as they were looking for answers.

Black Death / "Bubonic Plague"

Commonly known as the "bubonic plague," the Black Death of 1350 was another significant pandemic that killed approximately one-third of the world population during its time. It is said to have possibly started in Asia and moved west in caravans. People who had the disease, upon arriving at the Port of Messina in Sicily, Italy in 1347 A.D., rapidly spread the virus throughout Europe (Editors, 2021, December 21). One thing that is interesting about the bubonic plague is that something happened during this pandemic that mirrors what we learned through various news broadcasts during the COVID-19 pandemic — an overabundance of corpses created challenges for burial in the United States of America.

The Columbian Exchange

In 1492, another pandemic, named The Columbian Exchange, occurred. This pandemic, which consisted of smallpox, measles, and the bubonic plague, is said to have devastated the native people, with as many as 90 per cent dying throughout the northern and southern continents. Since these people were not previously exposed to these diseases, it is believed that the diseases were transmitted to the natives by the Europeans (Editors, 2021, December 21). What a tragic event to see a whole population nearly wiped out by illnesses.

Great Plague of London

The Great Plague of London in 1665, another virus deemed as the "bubonic plague," is recorded as the next pandemic that resulted in the deaths of 20 per cent of London's population. It was documented that as human death tolls increased, giving rise to mass graves, "hundreds of thousands of cats and dogs were slaughtered as the possible cause" of the disease (Editors, 2021, December 21). However, in the end, the worst of the outbreak of the pandemic tapered off in the fall of 1666, around the same time as another destructive event—the Great Fire of London (Editors, 2021, December 21). Between the plague and the fire, London suffered incredible losses during these short years. Many lost their homes, their loved ones, and parts of their city all at the same time.

Cholera

Then, in 1817, Russia experienced the Cholera Pandemic, the first of seven that occurred over the next 150 years. It is noted that this wave of the small intestine infection originated in Russia, where one million people died, and it was then passed along to British soldiers who brought it to India where millions of people died. The reach of the British Empire, and its navy, spread cholera to Spain, Africa, Indonesia, China, Japan, Italy, Germany, and America, resulting in the death of roughly 150,000 people. Although a vaccine was developed in 1885, the pandemic continued (Editors, 2021, December 21). After 7 different strands in 150 years and an ineffective vaccine, I'm sure people thought this pandemic would never end!

Third Plague Pandemic

A subsequent pandemic of 1855 known as the Third Plague Pandemic, is said to have started in China and moved to India and Hong Kong, where it claimed the lives of 15 million people. This pandemic was considered active until 1960 when cases dropped below a couple hundred. A few interesting facts about this pandemic are: 1) it is considered a factor in the Parthay rebellion and the Taiping rebellion; 2) India faced the most substantial casualties and 3) the pandemic was used as an excuse for repressive policies that sparked the revolt against the British (Editors, 2021, December 21).

Measles

In 1875, the Fiji Measles Pandemic emerged. History reveals that after Fiji surrendered to the British Empire, a royal party visited Australia as a gift from Queen Victoria. During this time, the royal party brought the disease to the island, and it was spread further by the tribal heads and police who met them upon their arrival. It is estimated that "one-third of Fiji's population, a total of 40,000 people, died" (Editors, 2021, December 21).

Russian Flu

In 1889, the Russian Flu, said to be the first significant flu pandemic, began in Siberia and Kazakhstan, travelled to Moscow, and then to Finland, followed by Poland, and after that, entered the rest of Europe. By the following year, 1890, it reached North America and Africa, where by the end of that year, approximately 360,000 people died (Editors, 2021, December 21).

Spanish Flu

The Spanish flu pandemic of 1918, recorded as "the deadliest in history," was believed to have infected an estimated "500 million people worldwide—about one-third of the planet's population—and killed an estimated 20 million to 50 million victims, including some 675,000 Americans" (Editors, 2020, May 19). This flu has been compared to the COVID-19 pandemic of our generation, where Fagunwa (2020) writes that "like the case of COVID-19, the pandemic of 1918 kept Christians, as well as people of other faiths, from worshipping together" (p. 52).

The Spanish flu is said to have been first observed in Europe, the United States, and parts of Asia, before swiftly spreading around the world. At that time, there were no effective drugs or vaccines to treat it. Like COVID-19 protocols, people were ordered to wear masks; schools, theatres, and businesses were closed; and bodies were contained in makeshift morgues (Editors, 2020, May 19).

Though this was 100 years before COVID-19, it is similar in nature, the fact that it occurred worldwide and no one was safe from getting it. Its rapid spread and high infection rate are what caused imposed quarantines, wearing of masks and locked-down of public places, including schools, churches, and theatres. People were also advised to avoid shaking hands and to stay indoors.

ASIAN FLU

After the Spanish flu pandemic, the Asian flu of 1957 appeared. It is said to have originated in Hong Kong, then spread throughout China and continued onto the United States. It then became widespread in England, where, over six months, 14,000 people died. In 1958, a second wave of the pandemic followed, which caused approximately 1.1 million deaths globally. 116,000 of said deaths occurred in the United States of America. However, a vaccine was soon developed that effectively contained the pandemic (Editors, 2021, December 21).

HIV / AIDS

HIV / AIDs is a recent phenomenon in our lifetime originating in the 1980s and early 1990s. It was reported that "an outbreak of this disease swept across the United States and the rest of the world, though the disease originated decades earlier" (Greene, WC 2007). Recent statistics documented that "more than 70 million people have been infected with HIV and about 35 million have died from AIDS since the start of the pandemic" (Editors, 2021, February 21).

SARS

SARS (severe acute respiratory syndrome) was the most recent worldwide pandemic, previous to COVID-19. It was believed to have started with bats, which spread to cats and then to humans in China and ultimately spread to 26 other countries. This virus was "first identified in 2003, after several months of cases, when 8,096 people were infected" (Editors, 2021, December 21). SARS caused "774 deaths" (Editors, 2021, December 21). It was stated that health professionals learned valuable medical information from this pandemic that was "used to keep diseases like H1N1, Ebola, and Zika under control" (Editors, 2021, December 21).

In Canada, specifically, we experienced an outbreak of SARS with most infections originating in hospitals in Toronto. The outbreak resulted in thousands of people being quarantined, several deaths, and an economic loss for Toronto (Rae & Zeng, 2006). SARS may be the precursor to the COVID-19 pandemic, but it was certainly not of the same magnitude.

COVID-19 "Coronavirus"

The COVID-19 pandemic, beginning in late 2019, is the latest of the pandemics that changed history. The impact of COVID-19 was severe, as people were forced to isolate themselves. The government enacted a "stay-at-home" legislation, to minimize transmission of the virus and prevent hospitals from becoming overpopulated.

It was on March 11, 2020, that the World Health Organization (WHO) announced that "the COVID-19 virus was officially a pandemic after barreling through 114 countries in three months and infecting over 118,000 people" and that "the spread wasn't anywhere near finished" (Editors, 2021, December 21). In the US, the government originally started with a two-week total lockdown, hoping the worst of the virus would be over by then and families could gather together again by Easter time. No one knew the magnitude of the situation or just how long the isolation period would last.

The first Ontario (Canada) province-wide shutdown took effect on Saturday, December 26, 2020, at 12:01 a.m. This meant the elimination of a favourite pastime, the early morning lineup of shoppers looking for Boxing Day sales. For those unfamiliar with "Boxing Day," it is similar to what "Black Friday" looks like in the US: the day to find the best deals of the year. One news headline read *"Ontario Announces Provincewide Shutdown to Stop Spread of COVID-19 and Save Lives"* (The Province of Ontario, Office of the Premier, 2020).

The Church was not exempt from the legislation imposed by the government. It too was forced to "cease physical assembling" under the Emergency Management and Civil Protection Act, R.S.O. 1990, c. E.9. The COVID-19 pandemic was equated to the Spanish Flu pandemic of 1918, which also kept people of faith from worshipping together (Fagunwa, 2020). Most of society today is unfamiliar with this pandemic because it happened over 100 years ago.

It was reported that COVID-19 spread to almost every country in the world, and that "by December 2020, it had infected more than 75 million people and led to more than 1.6 million deaths worldwide" (Editors, 2021, December 21). Today, globally, there are over 662 million COVID-19 cases and over 6 million deaths (World Health Organization, 2023, January 17).

As I write this book, the world is still experiencing COVID-19. Although, great improvements have been made to lessen its impact on society. The most notable preventative measures available are vaccination, wearing of face masks, and social distancing of 6 feet (or 2 meters) apart. During this time, the Canadian government is offering its fourth "shot" of the COVID-19 vaccine.

PANDEMIC AFTERMATH

This array of pandemics wreaked havoc on societies in many different ways. It has resulted in economic downfalls, an escalated sense of fear and concern among society, and more. The largest impact is, obviously, the devastation that comes along with the number of deaths and infections caused. I believe the result is best encapsulated in one theme — an overwhelmingly negative effect on society during each period of occurrence. What we can recognize from this chapter is that we are not the first to experience devastating events like these. Those before us were struck with the same heartache, fears, and confusion that we had. They too questioned the significance of these situations and wondered if life would ever return to "normal."

REFLECTIONS

Chapter Two:
The Church's Response

During these times of sickness and turmoil, how did God's people respond? As we look at the Church's response, it should cause us to consider how we responded personally as well. Did we let fear overcome us? Did we act selfishly out of concern for ourselves or did we demonstrate the selfless love of Christ? It's important to keep in mind that we are each a part of the body of Christ and we play a significant role in sharing the love of Jesus with others. We cannot sit idly by during hard times and leave it to the church leaders alone to demonstrate the love of God.

As much as we desire to respond to situations with love and grace, sometimes our reactions to stressful circumstances, such as the pandemic, are not ideal. For instance, I discovered during my research that non-Christlike behaviours—such as divisiveness, anger, complaining, rudeness, impatience, defiance, and selfishness—were exhibited by Christians as well.

In times of struggle, the community will observe how the Church responds. As a foundation that proclaims love, they will look to see how people within the Church respond when push comes to shove. Will they act in consideration for others or out of concern for themselves? In this chapter, we'll examine the Church's response to pandemics in two separate categories: how the Church responded to previous pandemics, and how the church responded during the COVID-19 pandemic.

COVID-19 is a unique pandemic that presented the church with challenges it hadn't faced in the past. It also brought about unique opportunities. The response of the Church during this pandemic reflects some similarities to historic responses, as well as various actions and outcomes. Historically, the response of the Christian Church has been remarkably positive overall, despite a few negative occurrences. Two consistent attributes of the Church's response, even during COVID-19, were that the Church, as a whole, never truly closed and that Church leaders continued to play significant roles in their community.

Church Response to Previous Pandemics

Throughout history, the Church has shown great compassion during pandemics. They ministered to the sick and dying, making no distinction between Christians and non-Christians. They provided relevant services to everyone in need. This response to pandemic outbreaks was provided by the church leaders and parishioners, a feat that was described as "connecting their service to martyrdom" (Just, 2020, p. 8). Providing care for the sick and dying during a pandemic was "thought of as a revolutionary concept in the ancient world" but research shows that it "became characteristic of Christians" (Just, 2020, p. 8). The church leaders put others before themselves, risking their own lives, to provide care and pastoral services to those affected. They became the visible hands and feet of Jesus during the pandemic, living out the same type of love that Christ showed for us in John 15:13: *"Greater love has no one than this, than to lay down one's life for his friends."*

PLAGUE OF CYPRIAN

During the Plague of Cyprian — 250 A.D., Cyprian, the Bishop of Carthage, called on citizens, both Christians and non-Christians, to help their neighbours in caring for the sick and burying the dead. More specifically, Cyprian did not ignore the crisis, but instead, encouraged Christians to risk their own lives to care for the vulnerable. Cyprian requested money from the rich and services from the poor. He encouraged Christians not to make any distinction between caring for fellow Christians and caring for pagans. He believed that everyone should receive care, even those who actively persecuted the Church (Just, 2020). He called on Christians to put Matthew 5:44 into action: "*But I say to you, love your enemies, bless those who curse you, do good to those who hate you, and pray for those who spitefully use you and persecute you.*" Jesus used this verse to challenge religious leaders' perspectives on who they should love, urging them to not only offer their love to those who love them, but to their enemies as well. It was this same logic that Cyprian applied to care for those in need throughout this plague.

COMPASSION OF CHRISTIANS

A decade later, it was recorded that Bishop Dionysius of Alexandria observed the contrast between the actions of Christians and pagans during the plague. He found that many pagans abandoned the vulnerable, while Christians showed love and compassion for them. This resulted in pagans being drawn to the Church because of the noticeably selfless actions of Christians (Gonzalez, 2020). Christians during this time took to heart Jesus' words in Matthew 5:16 "*Let your light so shine before men, that they may see your good works and glorify your Father in heaven.*" They were an example of selflessness and love to many who had never known it, to those who hadn't done anything to earn their favour.

Dionysius explained that throughout the second and third centuries, the Church created local structures to lessen the task of helping the vulnerable. They provided food, clothing, and money, cared for the sick, and comforted those who were near death. These actions were considered essential characteristics of what it meant to be the Church. The bishop was seen as a leader, and it was believed that he "probably set the tone" for the effective delivery of these services, which are now often provided by the Church (Gonzalez, 2020, p. 16).

Dionysius, upon observing the actions taken by Cyprian, Bishop of Carthage, said that "Cyprian was clearly a model for a graceful response to Christian and non-Christian alike when a situation like the pandemic occurred" (Gonzalez, 2020, p.16). Barnes (2020) also recorded Dionysius' observation of the Christian Church:

> *"Most of our brother-Christians showed unbounded love and loyalty, never sparing themselves and thinking only of one another. Heedless of the danger, they took charge of the sick, attending to their every need and ministering to them in Christ, and with them departed this life serenely happy; for they were infected by others with the disease, drawing on themselves the sickness of their neighbours and cheerfully accepting their pains. Cyprian understood Paul's warning against grieving like those without hope (l Thess. 4:13) to mean that Christians should not grieve at all"* (pp. 78-79).

Another Bishop, Eusebius of Caesarea, declared that the demonstration of care by Christians was not limited to the Cyprian plague. He referred to an epidemic lasting from 312— 313 A.D., stating:

"Christians, in the midst of such ills, showed their sympathy and humanity by their deeds. Every day some continued caring for and burying the dead, for there were multitudes who had no one to care for them" (Just, 2020, p. 8).

In addition, Eusebius said:

"Others collected in one place those who were afflicted by the famine, throughout the entire city, and gave bread to them all; so that the 'thing' became reported abroad among all men, and they glorified the God of the Christians" (Just, 2020, p. 8).

SPURGEON'S MINISTRY

The response of Charles Haddon Spurgeon, the famous English preacher known as the "Prince of Preachers," was also exemplary. He prioritized his community by focusing his efforts on local ministry and turning down all invitations to preach in other parts of the country. He committed to staying with his people, caring for the sick among them. Spurgeon, himself, wrote "family after family summoned me to the bedside of the smitten, and almost every day I was called to visit the grave" (Barnes, 2020, p. 91). During this time, Spurgeon was open to new evangelistic opportunities that presented themselves. He ministered to the sick by visiting their house to evangelize and comfort them. He entrusted his life to God, relying on Him as the source of strength to carry on his work, despite physical and mental exhaustion. He charged pastors and Christians to share the Gospel of Jesus Christ, bringing hope into the lives of others. Spurgeon also advocated on behalf of the poor, commanding greater cleanliness and better dwellings for them. He conducted medical research, to aid in the relief efforts, as well (Barnes, 2020).

Negative Responses

We have reviewed several testimonies of the selflessness of Christians during historical pandemics. While many leaders responded in the love of Christ, which is inspiring, we also need to acknowledge the other side of the spectrum of responses as well. As mentioned at the beginning of the chapter, there were a few recorded instances where the response of the Church to the pandemic was less than Christ-like.

One unfavourable trait that some Christians and Church leaders were guilty of was abandonment. Churchgoers were abandoned by their priests, as some priests refused to provide sacraments to the dying. Other church members abandoned their own families, out of selfishness or fear of falling ill (Gonzalez, 2020). This resulted in a deep hurt for those abandoned, as they were left by the ones closest to them, who they should have been able to rely on.

Another example of a negative action that took place in the Church is naming and blaming. Some church leaders, and their congregants, blamed God for the Black Death, "the Great Plague of the fourteenth century." In their view of this plague as divine intervention, they searched for answers as to who was to be blamed (Gonsalez, 2020, p. 18). Having no concrete evidence of who had brought this plague upon them, they implicated that the Jews, witches, and others were to blame (Gonsalez, 2020). This caused division and judgment among communities, as individuals blamed God and one another.

Christianity Demonstrated

Overall, the Christian Church responded tremendously positively to the pandemic outbreaks. The compassionate response of the Church during the early pandemics is believed to be the inspiration for the success of our modern hospital system: "when the concept of a hospital began to emerge in the mid-fourth century, it owed much to the church's long experience for caring for the ill . . . without [it] the immediate success of the hospital, I believe, would have been impossible" (Just, 2020, p. 9).

While there were a few exceptions, many Christians responded to these times of crisis with faith and compassion. They set a standard of what it looked like to care for others selflessly.

Church Response to COVID-19

The positive actions of the Church during the COVID-19 pandemic were comparable to those of the Church before COVID-19. This claim is based on findings from recent interviews. Interviews were conducted with seven church leaders (pastors and priests) from seven different denominations in December 2021 and January 2022. Data was also collected through an online survey of 100 congregants from these same denominations in January and February 2022. See Appendix A (p. 111) for a description of the denominations interviewed. This survey asked leaders and congregants a variety of questions regarding the pandemic and its effects.

We need to recognize that society is significantly different during this COVID-19 pandemic than it was in the pandemics preceding COVID-19. For example, during COVID-19, critical infrastructures like a robust healthcare system, numerous hospitals, various medical facilities, and large buildings that can be converted into temporary medical sites were in place, whereas, during worldwide pandemics before COVID-19, many of these amenities did not exist. Therefore, there will naturally be some variation of the response of the Church during COVID-19 from that of the Church before COVID-19.

The Call to Assemble

The government-ordered closure of church buildings presented a new challenge to bodies of faith during COVID-19. In previous pandemics, with the exception of the Spanish flu of 1918, churches were still permitted to meet together. However, that option was not available to the Church during COVID-19, because it was forced to close its doors. This highlights a significant difference in what church gatherings looked like during previous pandemics and COVID-19. The latter Church was forced to find another way to assemble that didn't involve a physical gathering.

The physical assembling of congregants is a core part of the Church, based on the Biblical teaching, "not forsaking the assembling of ourselves together…" (Heb. 10:25). Meeting together is a vital component in the life of believers, as it helps strengthen our faith in God while building a community of Christ-centered individuals. It allow us to sing praises to God in unison and participate in taking the sacraments (communion) together. Gathering with one another facilitates a vibrant and dynamic setting to experience unrestrained worship and immerse ourselves at a deeper level, where we can feel that we are in the presence of God. Weekly gatherings of believers have been a core aspect of the body of Christ since Biblical times. This is one reason why COVID-19 forced a change in the church.

ONLINE GATHERINGS

While the Church complied with the shutdown, it refused to give up the relational structure of meeting together, scrambling to find new ways to do so. Churches implemented technology to create an online format, giving members different options for "attending." They could meet together through scheduled video calls such as Zoom or Google Meet, or by watching live streams on platforms like Facebook and YouTube.

Congregants attended Church online (virtual church) instead of the traditional in-person gatherings they were used to. Church leaders also conducted Sunday School, Bible Study, prayer meetings, seminars, etc., online to minister to congregants and provide spiritual care. This gave members opportunities throughout the week to interact on a more personal level. One leader that I spoke to even launched a new discipleship program series that he spent two years developing. The program encouraged people to invest in their "own" discipleship and growth, which was deeply appreciated.

OTHER CONNECTION STRATEGIES

Of course, not every church was equipped with the technology necessary to stream services; therefore, these churches got creative and connected in other ways such as by telephone, drive-by visits, and other means which did not involve close contact with people.

On the congregant end, not every churchgoer had the means available (laptop, smartphone, smart tv, tablet, etc.) to participate in church online. The church closure had a more significant impact on this segment of the Church population, as they did not have access to weekly meetings with others in the body. This placed a heavy responsibility on church leaders to personally reach out to these individuals through phone calls or distanced non-contact visits.

Servant Leadership

Servant leadership was a key response by Church leaders during the pandemic. Fortin (2021) stated, "Christian leadership is servant leadership…." (p. 38). This kind of leadership, he also noted, "… is not exercised by imposing one person's, ideas, and policies on others, but rather by opening oneself up to reveal one's vulnerability" (p. 38).

The vulnerability of church leaders was evident, as they were thrust into an unfamiliar environment, being forced to adapt church services from in-person to virtual (online). They had to quickly learn how to function in this environment, with no instruction manual on how to do so. According to one leader, "We pivoted, and it was not so much a pivot. It was a kick or a pusher from out of the building…It was a hot mess; we had no idea." However, as Fortin (2021) also noted, "confrontation with real-life challenges forges a resilient personality able to discern and follow, in difficult situations and circumstances, the most faithful course of action" (p. 38). When faced with this unforeseen challenge, leaders took the most practical course of action using technology to deliver services online through mediums such as Zoom, Facebook, Twitter, Google Meet, and more.

They also implemented electronic giving, e-bulletins, and online announcements, to ensure that congregants could participate and stay updated as much as possible. They made use of email communication platforms to spread information to a large number of people at once. Congregations consisting of older generations, or members who were not tech-savvy, invoked existing phone trees or formulated new ones. More than ever, communication and connection in the church body were of the utmost importance.

Leaders also orchestrated community initiatives such as food drives and distribution. They welcomed visitors and assisted them as required. They found means to reach out and bring a sense of hope to the community by involving them in non-contact activities such as citywide scavenger hunts and other community events.

Overall, the Church during the COVID-19 Pandemic was adaptable, community-focused, and compassionate. The Church proved to be resilient and flexible, doing what it took to continue to spread the gospel when its usual means were taken away. Church leaders found ways to bring people together during this time apart.

Church Leaders and The Vaccine

The vaccine is a topic that caused a lot of discussion and discord among society and within the Church. It was controversial, in the fact that most either felt strongly in support of it or strongly against it. There was a significant amount of resistance in society to the COVID-19 vaccine, which was heightened due to a lack of trust. This is based primarily on the belief of many that it was an untested or experimental vaccine. This skepticism seeped into the

Church, with congregants using Scriptures to justify not getting vaccinated against the COVID virus. Therefore, this was one area where the Church became divided against itself, resulting in the need for leaders to exercise sound leadership and take bold actions. Many congregants looked to their pastors and church leaders during this time for guidance and answers.

Based on my research, the Church leaders stepped up, responding courageously to the pressure they were under. The leaders' responses were robust and varied in the course of actions taken.

Vaccine Support

Several church leaders supported the vaccine efforts and boldly demonstrated this to their congregation. Some acted in advisory roles for the vaccine, such as being on the mayor's committee (Mayor of Toronto); some leaders built vaccine confidence among congregants through education, while others supported congregants as vaccine ambassadors to help more people become vaccinated with the hope of slowing the spread of the COVID-19 virus. Church leaders promoted the interdependency of the Church to the people and the people to the Church in order to help congregants build and maintain their faith in God. They worked to dispel myths and misinformation about the pandemic, in hopes to alleviate expressed fear and concern.

One leader disclosed her vaccination status as soon as she was vaccinated to show her support for the vaccine, saying she felt "it was an answer to her prayer." Another, in his own way, disclosed to the congregation that he and his family had been vaccinated. He made known to them that he believed in the science of the vaccine and had done thorough research. Furthermore, he was affiliated with people who had strong healthcare backgrounds, who were in full support of this action. This reassured him in the fact that he and his family were making a wise decision. Though he believed strongly in the validity of the vaccine, he maintained that he would not try to influence his congregation. Rather, he would provide them with information to make the best decision for themselves and their families.

Another leader felt that his influence was by example, set by the attitude that the leadership in his Church showed to its congregants. He also believed that the Scriptures teach that we should submit to our authorities, except when they ask us to violate the commands of Scripture. Therefore, he thought that his church demonstrated a respectful and submissive tone toward authorities. He believed that this viewpoint positively influenced his congregation's attitude toward the vaccine, at some level.

CONGREGATIONAL RESPECT AND UNITY

Another man in Church leadership expressed that he made it "very clear, at the very beginning," that he "was not going to police this issue." He felt that he was not "called to be a police officer," but was instead "called to be a pastor." As a result, he decided not to judge people but to adopt a balanced approach where he diligently "looked at both sides of the aisle regarding the vaccine: pro-vaccine and anti-vaccine." This leader trusted the members of his congregation to make the decision that they saw fit for themselves and treat others on the opposite side of the argument with respect.

One of the leaders explained that his denomination encouraged responsible immunization and did not have any religious or faith-based reason to refrain from vaccination. He didn't see any reason not to encourage his members to responsibly participate in protective and preventive immunization programs. He also shared that his denomination does not tell a member "You must be vaccinated" or "You should not be vaccinated." Instead, his denomination highlights the importance of life, community health, and the need to demonstrate the compassion of Christ.

Another participant expressed that he had not spoken about the vaccination from the pulpit, as he felt that he should not be speaking about vaccinations from this platform. However, if someone asked him specifically, he would disclose his vaccination status, which in his case, he was vaccinated.

One leader demonstrated great responsibility and diligence, by creating a weekly blog and YouTube segment. Through this blog, he addressed different topics from Scriptures: primarily, commonly misused Scriptures used to influence people against being vaccinated. In his posts, he brought up comments such as, "Oh just trust God, don't bother with medicine or anything like that." This same leader also wrote an article titled, "Should a Christian Get Vaccinated or Trust God to Protect Them from COVID-19?" in which he highlighted Psalm 91 as a premier Scripture that people use as "assurance of God's protection against COVID-19." For example: *"You shall not be afraid of the terror by night, Nor of the arrow that flies by day, Nor of the pestilence that walks in darkness, Nor of the destruction that lays waste at noonday,"* (Psalm 91:5-6) and *"Because you have made the LORD, who is my refuge, Even the Most High, your dwelling place, No evil shall be befall you, Nor shall any plague come near your dwelling"* (Psalm 91:9-10).

Lastly, one leader summed up his action in a sound bite that was posted on a sign at the front of his church that said, "Get vaccinated; share God's love."

While some church leaders were not fond of the idea of the vaccine, the majority of those interviewed were supportive of it. At the least, they were respectful of the medical efforts that went into it, and encouraged their congregants to do their own research, making thoughtful decisions for their families.

Church Collaboration

During this time when individuals had to be physically alone, it became more important than ever to demonstrate that they were not on their own. The Church is not several separate entities, but one united body of Christ. Church leaders demonstrated positive collaborative involvement with other local churches, including: providing financial assistance to affiliate congregations, helping to facilitate fundraisers for other congregations, and allowing other congregations to observe and learn from their operations.

Church Involvement in Community

In this period of isolation, the Church had an opportunity to be a beacon of hope and a shining example of God's love to a community that was hurting, as it had during previous pandemics. While the church doors were not open during COVID-19, as they have been in the past, the presence of the Church in the community was still made known.

In my research to find out how the Church was viewed in terms of the support it provided to communities, congregants were asked through an online survey to indicate "yes" or "no" if they believed the Church had been a source of support and help to communities during the pandemic and provide a reason for their choice. Table 1 summarizes the responses:

Table 1

Congregants' View of the Church as a Source of Support to Communities

Yes	No
85%	15%

The survey concluded an overwhelmingly positive result. Respondents who believed the Church had been a source of support and help to communities during the pandemic concluded that the Church represented itself well and did what was expected of the Church. Specifics responses were:

"Being a tower of strength for people — mentally, physically, and emotionally"

"Using technology such as Zoom, YouTube, Twitter, Facebook livestream, and teleconference to deliver services such as online church, small groups, prayer meetings"

"Providing shower and laundry services"

"Providing financial assistance"

"Creating food hubs and drives"

"Delivering food boxes"

"Comforting people who were experiencing loss of loved ones"

"Providing telephone counseling"

"Maintaining policies and guidelines for covid protection"

"Distributing personal protective equipment (PPE)"

"Educating congregants"

"Providing support to communities"

"Being present throughout the pandemic"

One respondent observed the impact firsthand, saying,

"I have seen their actions and [positive] results that happened"

Those who expressed that the Church was not a source of support believed that the help provided by the church was limited, as some churches did not provide any support. Some respondents also said that more could have been done to encourage individuals to seek God on a deeper level in these times, rather than focus on the vaccine. Some noted that more effort to reach congregants online would have been appreciated.

THE CHURCH'S EMERGENCY RESPONSE

I had the interview participants recall the "9/11 Tragedy," the destruction of the World Trade Center in New York, U.S.A. In doing this, I wanted to find out the leaders' thoughts in drawing a comparison between the tragedy and the pandemic. Therefore, I asked them if they believed the church was a source of support during this pandemic as much as it was during the aftermath of 9/11.

Responses were mixed, consisting of "yes," "no," and "somewhat." The main reason given was the stark difference between the two phenomena. For instance, during 9/11, churches were open for all people to attend, while, with the pandemic, churches were closed, preventing people from attending. While it was easy to look to the Church for support during 9/11 for the mere fact that churches were open, that was not the case with the pandemic because churches were locked down by order of the government. Though church services became easily accessible online during the pandemic, there is something to be said about having a physical presence in a community to draw people in off the street. During the aftermath of 9/11, church buildings were open as a safe place for people to come and grieve, a place they could be physically comforted.

Another key observation that the leaders presented was the increase in church attendance rising as a result of 9/11 versus the decline in church attendance due to the pandemic. They also noted the increase in secularization in society during COVID-19. Despite efforts of the church to pivot to online services to meet the needs of the people, just as it did during 9/11, church attendance decreased significantly. One leader expressed that the reason for this difference was that 9/11 had a definitive ending, whereas COVID-19 is still ongoing and appears to not have an absolute ending. This results in huge obstacles to meeting and being with each other—even for those at the core of our churches.

Based on my findings, the actions taken by the leaders were parallel to those taken by church leaders during previous pandemics. The Church took an unexpected and challenging situation and rose to the occasion to make a positive impact, spreading hope among all the uncertainty. I believe their actions can be encapsulated in this statement by Barnes (2020): they "showed unbounded love and loyalty, never sparing themselves and thinking only of one another" (p. 78).

"By this all will know that you are My disciples, if you have love for one another."

John 13:35

REFLECTIONS

Chapter Three:
Change in Activities During the Pandemic

Sometimes, changes in our lives force us to come to terms with reality. They can require a paradigm shift and force us to make tough decisions. COVID-19 shook up life as we knew it and forced us to do things differently, most notably wearing face masks and staying socially distanced. All of a sudden, our ordinary routines were shaken up and we had to change the way we did things. We could no longer go out without wearing masks, we had to limit family gatherings to immediate family members, and we could no longer invite friends over, for fear of contracting or spreading the COVID-19 virus. For these reasons, many of us had to alter the way we engaged in everyday activities. I surveyed congregants to see what their experience with these changes was like by asking five different questions regarding activities that changed significantly, in format or occurrence, throughout COVID-19. The results show an interesting impact that this virus had on churches, which could also signify a change in the course of the future of the Church.

Church Participation During the Pandemic

My first question regarding the change in these individuals' lives during COVID-19 was regarding church participation. The following table gives an overview of participants' responses to the question: "How did you participate in church while the church was officially closed?" 100 people were surveyed, but they were able to check more than one answer, as many people participated in more than one of the following formats.

Table 2

Methods of Participating in Church During the Closure of the Church

Methods	Number of Respondents
Zoom	61
YouTube	40
Facebook	26
Small Group Meetings with Friends	13
Small Group Meetings with Family	6
None of the Above	12
Other (e.g., livestream, Facebook Messenger, Church Website)*	1

1 for each option

As the table indicates, Zoom emerged as the most popular method for attending virtual (online) church, followed by YouTube, and then Facebook. Who would have thought a few years back that it would become normal to login to a computer to "attend" church?

Non-Church Activity Participation During the Pandemic

Besides attending church through online formats, I wanted to find out what other activities people were still participating in. Respondents were asked to identify other activities in which they participated during the pandemic and could select from these options indicated in Table 3:

Table 3

Congregants' Involvement in Other Activities During the Pandemic

Other Activities	Number of Respondents
Go to the Movies	10
Visit Friends	39
Take Day Trips	28
Go to Parties	6
Volunteering	29
Return to School Online	13
Gardening	27

Learn a New Skill or Trade	11
Go to the Mall	32
None of the Above	15
Other (Work)	2
Other (e.g., exercise, read, watch T.V., walk, relax, Zoom visits)*	1

*_1 (1%) for each option_

There were several closings and re-openings of public places throughout the pandemic, which allowed people to occasionally participate in activities such as going to the movies and the mall, visiting friends, and taking day trips. Of course, once there was a full-scale lockdown, none of these activities were allowed as there was a law in place and violators could be charged for breaking it. This data is in reference to the time before the complete government-ordered lockdown. At this time, people were being cautious as they were aware of the virus, but they were not yet restricted from activities.

VIRTUAL CHURCH VISITS DURING THE PANDEMIC

With a plethora of church services becoming readily available online, it opened up options during the pandemic, for people to make virtual (online) visits to other churches that they did not regularly attend. I asked the congregants if they attended other churches online during COVID-19 and table 4 summarizes their responses.

Table 4

Virtual Visits by Congregants to Other Churches During the Pandemic

Yes	No
46%	54%

It is interesting to note that, although the majority of respondents did not make virtual visits to other churches, almost half of the churchgoers surveyed did. With the tendency of many congregants to change churches, I wonder how many of the 46% of respondents may have been influenced to leave their existing church and attend another, after the reopening of the Church, based on their virtual visits during the pandemic. It also makes me wonder how many would have actually visited these other churches in person without having seen the livestream first. The opportunity to "visit" another church has never been easier! You can do so without stepping foot in an unfamiliar building, without being greeted by strangers, and you can stay as long, or as short, as you wish. This is an outcome of COVID-19 that has changed the approach of "church shopping" or "church hopping" dramatically. Anyone looking to attend a new church can first view their service online, to get a feel for the worship and preaching style before physically attending service.

Witnessing During the Pandemic

With the amount of confusion surrounding COVID-19 and the uncertainty it brought, there was a huge opportunity for believers to witness to others the unwavering hope that comes from Jesus. As Christians, we are called to share the truth of the gospel with others, but it doesn't always feel natural or convenient and sometimes we can make excuses as to why we are not doing so. Not being able to gather physically with others made the means of witnessing more limited. I was curious to see what percentage of survey participants were still actively witnessing throughout the pandemic and asked them to give me a reason why or why not. Table 5 gives a synopsis of the responses.

Table 5

Congregants Witnessing about Jesus Christ During the Pandemic

Yes	No
67%	33%

The survey shows that ⅔ of respondents claimed to be actively sharing the gospel throughout the pandemic, while ⅓ admitted that they had not been. Let's examine their reasoning for this:

Congregants who responded that they _witnessed_ gave the following reasons:

"Profession allows one to witness"

"Love for Jesus"

"A precious opportunity to witness the mandate"

"Duty of every Christian to tell others / someone about Jesus Christ and his love"

"Jesus asks us to share His love with others and no pandemic should stop that"

"Jesus is our anchor"

"Jesus is still delivering, healing, etc."

"Jesus is the answer to all our questions and confusion, the plan of God has not changed because there is a pandemic, and we should always be witnessing"

Respondents who indicated that they <u>did not witness</u> offered these responses:

"Significant reduction in interaction with people"

"Desire to not pretend to have the answers about the pandemic"

"Having the knowledge from a healthcare background that we were well overdue for a pandemic and therefore, it is not a surprise that one has occurred"

"Belief that one's own spiritual journey is their own to make and not to be imposed on others"

"Belief that witnessing is best done in person - people do not want to discuss religion - it is not necessary - we live in a Christian atmosphere and thus, we are all witnesses"

"Jesus is shown through our actions and who we are"

"Did not want to"

"No time due to the need to care for ill family members"

"Allow people to do their praying"

"Work in a Christian environment and do not have significant relationships with nonbelievers"

"Timidity to do so"

"Lack of knowledge for effective witnessing"

"Limited ability for outreach to address the pandemic"

"Confined by the pandemic"

"Stressed at times"

"Talking about religion can result in 'fights'"

What a smorgasbord of responses! 67% of the churchgoers interviewed continued to witness to others about Jesus, even when the traditional forms of meeting together were taken away from them. They got creative, and took the call to witness seriously, sharing their love for Jesus and those around them, through the encounters they had. Their tenacity to witness when it would have been easy to make an excuse not to do so is inspiring. It reminds me of the Apostle Paul in the Bible, who was faithful to preach the Gospel unashamedly, whatever his situation. He preached through great opposition and was even a witness from a prison cell. In Ephesians 6, he asks the church to pray for him, "...that I may open my mouth boldly to make known the mystery of the gospel" (v. 19). What a powerful thing to pray for! As Christians called to share the love of Jesus, this prayer should be in the heart of each of us.

FINANCIAL GIVING DURING THE PANDEMIC

While money is not the most popular subject to talk about, and often makes people uncomfortable, receiving tithes and offerings is a primary tenet of the Church, being its main source of income. It is believed that many churches experienced a financial loss due to a reduction in giving, stemming from the pandemic. One source aptly noted, "through the Churches Helping Churches Initiative, a relief fund has been set up to provide $3,000 grants to churches at risk of closing this spring due to a decrease in financial giving" (Molina, 2020, p. 17); and furthermore, "many small churches don't have hefty savings accounts or large annual incomes and rely heavily or solely on weekly offerings" (Molina, 2020, p. 17).

Molina (2020) also advised that National Christian groups urge larger and more stable churches to help small churches financially, churches that could potentially close due to a significant decline in tithes and offerings resulting from the pandemic.

I wanted to find out if congregants held firm to the principle of tithing throughout the pandemic, so I asked them to disclose if they gave tithes and offerings while the church building was closed during the pandemic. I then asked that they provide a reason for whether they did or didn't. Table 6 summarizes the responses.

Table 6

Giving of Tithes and Offerings by Congregants During the Pandemic

Yes	No
78%	22%

Nearly 80% of the congregation continued to give faithfully during the pandemic. A predominant reason provided for giving tithes and offerings was in regard to the requirement for the continuance of the operational needs of the church. A church's expenses don't just disappear because people temporarily aren't using the physical building.

Other responses included:

"Our responsibility"

"The importance of keeping a revenue stream for the church"

"A test of our (my) love for God, who gave me (us)
90% of His all"

"The importance of compensating ministers and staff"

"Obedience to God"

In addition, it was expressed that a pandemic does not change the commandment to pay tithes and offerings. Some referenced the command in verses such as Malachi 3:8: *"Will a man rob God? Yet you have robbed Me! But you say, 'In what way have we robbed You?' In tithes and offerings."* Others expressed that church expenses remain the same or greater, and tithes are a form of worship that indicates that the church must continue to exist.

Responses of those who did not pay tithes or offerings included not being able to get to the church, not knowing how to do so, not thinking about it, experiencing "hardship," loss of job, not working, and not being inclined due to laziness. I appreciate the honesty of the responses across the board. It helps us evaluate the effect on the Church's finances during the pandemic.

LEADER THOUGHTS ON THE FINANCIAL STATE OF THE CHURCH

I also wanted to hear the leaders' perspective on finances, so I inquired about the fiscal impact on their churches due to the pandemic. For this topic, I focused on three specific areas: assisting another church during the pandemic, financial adversity that could impact the future operations of their churches, and commitment to assist another church post-pandemic. The leaders were requested to provide reasons for their responses.

Overall, the consensus was that the Church was doing well financially. For the majority, governance structures within denominations allow for self-sufficiency. For example, some respondents explained that their governance structures provide for larger churches to support smaller churches. Another expressed that each church has its financial structure, and each congregation is financially sustainable, eliminating the need for churches to assist each other, except in joint ventures, where congregations are leading a ministry together for community work. In this instance, congregations would develop a joint budget.

Where assistance was required, churches stepped up to help other churches in the following ways: assisting affiliate churches financially, helping to facilitate fundraisers, and allowing other congregations to observe their processes such as live streaming, camera operations, and online administration procedures.

In the cases where assistance was not provided, it was for reasons such as associated churches having healthy financial positions or churches not asking for or requiring assistance.

In terms of financial adversity that could impact the future operation of churches, the responses among all leaders consistently indicated they did not foresee any major future impact on operations. Nevertheless, one leader expressed a caveat that although its future operations are not impacted, "offerings were cut down by at least half." Another leader shared his experience implying that the larger churches seemed to be the ones that were struggling more financially than the smaller churches.

When we take a look at some of the leaders' responses, it should bolster the confidence of the Church concerning its relevance in society today. It should also reassure us of God's provision over the Church and His people during times of crisis. Here are a few of the leaders' reactions:

- "In our case, this is actually where God showed up in a shocking way, because we did well financially in the pandemic;"

- "In fact, our tithes and offerings generally grew in the pandemic time, because of the financial system we have whereby we approach our financial contributions to the church from a theological, Biblical point of view where you are encouraged to return a tenth of your earning and additional offering."

- "… so, we are running at least 90% of our pre-pandemic revenue, and our expenses are probably down more than 10%. That is what I have heard consistently from the churches with which we are associated."

Of the minority that expressed less healthy financial positions, one leader said that the organization had been in a decline mode regarding financial resources, pre-pandemic and during the pandemic. It was an ongoing issue at the church that he leads. However, he concluded on a positive note that the financial position of his church during the second year of the pandemic was much better than the first year.

Another leader shared his experience, saying his church planned to rethink the management of funds by re-budgeting and re-planning to accommodate other pandemic expenses. He also indicated that delaying some planned projects could help lift the financial burden.

When I asked the leaders if they would commit to helping another church, because of severe challenges arising from the pandemic, all of them responded affirmatively. One leader also highlighted that his denomination has its structure of helping each other. Another indicated that his church is committed to giving away twenty per cent of any money that is donated. While a third leader mentioned that his church has focused on giving more on a national level since the pandemic began than was done previously. This was in response to the requests they received.

Another leader explained that, in addition to supporting local churches, his denomination also conducted considerable mission-ary work. This work included assisting churches in particular communities here in Toronto. The impact this mission work had was visibly evident in many communities. Lastly, another leader reinforced the need to help as one of the lessons learned from the pandemic is "when problems arise, you are there to help." He was committed to helping, as it demonstrated love for each other, which is "one of the hallmarks or characteristics of the church." We see this in the New Testament Church in Acts. The people acted as one unit, caring for one another and sharing everything they had with each other so that no one was left in need.

"Now the multitude of those who believed were of one heart and one soul; neither did anyone say that any of the things he possessed was his own, but they had all things in common. And with great power the apostles gave witness to the resurrection of the Lord Jesus. And great grace was upon them all. Nor was there anyone among them who lacked; for all who were pos-sessors of lands or houses sold them, and brought the proceeds of the things that were sold, and laid them at the apostles' feet; and they distributed to each as anyone had need."

Acts 4:32-35

The leaders' responses to helping out faith communities that were struggling reflect the examples of the early church. We saw this same attitude in the church in Galatia, where it was said, *"Bear one another's burdens, and so fulfill the law of Christ"* (Gal. 6:2). These churches are demonstrating the reality of acting as one family, united through the blood of Jesus. Though church finances were impacted by COVID-19, leaders rose to the occasion to adjust budgets as necessary and be generous in giving to others in need.

REFLECTIONS

Chapter Four:
Congregants' Feelings Regarding COVID-19

As the pandemic brought about many questions, people started speculating as to why it occurred or what it could signify. I heard several different reasons being tossed about for its existence. The one that caught my attention most was the pandemic being associated with the fulfillment of Biblical prophecy. This led me to explore the topic further by asking congregants if they thought this pandemic was a sign of prophecy being fulfilled, specifically about the end time described in Matthew 24:7-8. These verses state, "... *there will be famines, pestilences, and earthquakes in various places. All these are the beginning of sorrows.*" As discussed in the introduction to this book, "pestilence" is another term for a pandemic. I wanted to find out if congregants saw the COVID-19 pandemic as one of these pestilences referred to. I asked them if they viewed it as a sign of the beginning of the end times. The following table illustrates the congregants' opinions on this matter.

Table 7

Congregants' View of the Pandemic: Fulfillment of Prophecy or Not

Yes	No
52%	48%

Congregants who responded "yes" believe that the pandemic was a sign of Biblical prophecy being fulfilled. They provided specific reasons for their responses, many that referenced Matthew 24, and the belief that COVID-19 was part of the "beginning of sorrows." They also stated the following beliefs:

"It is the commencing of a one-world system that is creating the stage for the Antichrist and the suffocation of civil liberties (in democratic, free-thinking societies)".

"Confirmation of Scriptures that allude to illnesses and diseases with the second coming of Christ, and a representation of the imminent return of Christ".

Congregants who responded "no" indicated feelings of uncertainty about the origins of the virus, feelings of the virus being manufactured ("man-made"), the belief of the virus originating from a new mutant virus, an acknowledgment that pandemics are natural and unfortunate occurrences that have happened before, history records pandemics, and the lack of scriptures to support such assumption.

Interestingly enough, the church was fairly evenly split on this matter. The fact that over half of the congregation believes the pandemic to be fulfilling a part of the end-time prophecy should at least put it on the radar of all believers. End times or not, it is important for us to consider if our daily lives are reflecting the belief that Jesus is coming back. Does the way that we are living today demonstrate this reality? If we knew the end was near, what would we do differently? Perhaps, we would witness more intentionally to our friends and family. Maybe we would prioritize a right relationship with God, instead of just getting by. Knowing the end is coming should cause us to think seriously about our mission and our impact on this world.

In Acts 1:7-8, just before Jesus leaves his disciples to ascend into Heaven, he gives them these final words, "...*It is not for you to know times or seasons which the Father has put in His own authority. But you shall receive power when the Holy Spirit has come upon you; and you shall be witnesses to Me in Jerusalem, and in all Judea and Samaria, and to the end of the earth.*" While none of us can know for certain the day or the hour that Jesus will return, our call to witness to others, with the confidence that he is returning, remains the same.

THE VACCINE AS THE ANTIDOTE

When the COVID-19 vaccine was developed, it became a hot topic, with lots of speculation revolving around it. I encountered people on both sides of the fence on this matter, as I'm sure we all have. I wanted to see, out of the congregants interviewed, which percentage believed the vaccine had helped to reduce the spread of the COVID-19 virus and which percentage did not. I then asked both sides to elaborate on the reason for their choice. Table 8 shows their responses.

Table 8

Congregants' View of the COVID-19 Vaccine: Antidote or Not

Yes	No
70%	30%

Participants that responded "yes" expressed the following sentiments:

"All vaccines help with many different diseases"

"The vaccine was responsible for the reduction in case counts based on available data"

"It lessened the severity and symptoms of the virus"

"Vaccinated people were less likely to be hospitalized, and if hospitalized the time spent in ICU was shorter"

In addition, they expressed support for science and its accomplishment of saving more lives through vaccination.

Individuals that responded "no" believed that the vaccine was ineffective, expressing the following:

"The effect on the human body is not known"

"The number of infected persons after receiving the vaccine states a case for itself"

"It does not reduce the spread of the virus and was ineffective against the 'Omicron' strain, for example"

Several of these "no" respondents also believed that the virus can still be transmitted by people who were vaccinated, making the appeal of the vaccine seem irrelevant.

With 70% of people interviewed believing the vaccine helped prevent the spread of the virus and 30% skeptical of its effect, the church was clearly divided on the topic, creating issues of unity within the body. When we have disagreements with our brothers and sisters in Christ, it is important that we refocus our attention on the core Biblical beliefs that unite us.

REFLECTIONS

Chapter Five:
The Return to "In-Person" Service

CONGREGANTS' FEELINGS ABOUT COVID-19 AND RETURN TO CHURCH

After such a long time apart, that felt as if it would never end, church buildings are now open under pandemic guidelines, such as social distancing. While many congregants have been eager to get back into the habit of meeting together, others are a little more hesitant. I asked participants to disclose if they have returned to in-person church services. The following table summarizes the responses.

Table 9

Status of Congregants as It Relates to Return to In-Person Church

Yes	No
48%	52%

We can see from these results that the majority of respondents have not returned to the traditional format of in-person church. Though the percentage is not significant over those who have returned, the fact that less than half of the congregation has returned is a bit surprising. Based on the tradition of the Church to assemble together, one might have expected that a greater number of congregants would have returned.

The results of this survey caused me to wonder what is holding people back from returning to Church. Is it their concern about the virus spreading through gathering together in a church building again or is it that congregants have become used to, and perhaps, fond of, the ease of a virtual church?

The next question asked congregants if they had concerns about returning to in-person church services. The participants were asked to respond "yes" or "no" and then provide reasons for their selection. The responses can be found in the following table:

Table 10

Concerns of Congregants about Returning to In-Person Church

Yes	No
30%	70%

The predominant response, as indicated in Table 10, was "no," indicating that most people did not have concerns about the virus in regard to returning to church services.

The three primary reasons provided for this response were: belief in one's immune system, belief that this flu strain was "way overblown - not a pandemic in the true sense," and the idea of maintaining traditions while doing so in a safe domain. Many welcomed the opportunity to meet again and considered it to be relatively low risk.

On the other hand, the minority who answered "yes" provided several responses that included these concerns:

"People demonstrating a lack of respect for the need for space and protection"

"People who do not adhere to safety protocols such as washing hands, wearing masks, remaining isolated if they suspect they might have the virus, and coughing in public spaces"

"The sanitation process of churches, including sanitizers at every pew"

"Contracting the virus"

"Protection of the elderly"

"Health issues of loved ones"

"Being in an enclosed space for some time with a large group of people"

"Residual pandemic paranoia"

While the majority of the survey respondents did not show concern about returning to in-person services, some held valid reservations about the issue of health among the congregation. Those who had compromising health concerns, or with loved ones who did, exercised more caution regarding which public spaces they entered. The answers imply that those hesitant about returning could not fully rely on the rest of the congregation to adhere to the distancing guidelines or refrain from attending at any signs of illness. They also wanted assurance that the church facility staff had done their due diligence to thoroughly disinfect rooms and surfaces and provide ample disinfecting supplies to the congregants.

One interesting takeaway from these results is that the percentage that had not yet returned to church was 52%, while those who admitted having concerns about returning was only 30%. This leaves a gap in the congregation consisting of people who have not returned for a reason other than health concerns. What is their reason for not returning? Do they plan to return at all?

"In-Person" Versus Online Service

With online church services becoming the norm during the pandemic and outweighing the alternative of not attending church at all, we got used to the virtual format. Now, with churches reopening, we may find ourselves wondering, do they offer the same experience or a different one entirely? Congregants were asked if they believed that in-person and virtual (online) services gave the same church experience. They were instructed to respond "yes" or "no" and provide a reason for their selection.

Table 11

Comparing Virtual and In-Person Church Experience

Yes	No
12%	88%

As seen in Table 11, the vast majority of participants responded "no," meaning that online and in-person did not provide the same experience. These congregants expressed that in-person service:

"Allows for better fellowshipping with others"

"Shows obedience to God who commanded us to celebrate mass and receive communion instead of watching it"

"Facilitates a feeling of community and connectedness"

They mentioned additional factors as well, saying,

"The gathering of the brethren is necessary for various needs of the congregants"

"One is easily distracted online"

"Virtual service feels like watching television"

and

"One cannot receive the eucharist online"

They also stated that the presence of God is felt more in "God's house," referring to the church building. They expanded on this point, declaring,

"There is a need to sing and pray together";

"Nothing can replace or come remotely close to the in-person experience";

"The online experience is 'definitely' lacking, and we should not forsake the general assembling of the church";

"There is a different 'energy' in the church; it is a pristine environment and helps one to 'cleanse' their aura";

"There is something magical about being in the building for service";

and,

"Home is not a church".

The 12% of respondents who answered "yes," meaning that virtual (online) gives the same church experience as in-person, stated that *both* provide "the same service and grace." They argued the point that "there is human contact and accountability for similar engagement when one's camera is turned on" and claimed that virtual service "bridges the gap for those not attending, as it creates an opportunity for everyone to get to see and hear each other, which is a form of contact." Those who advocated that online church gives the same experience were fans of the sense of virtual community that it manifested, while eliminating the risk of spreading illnesses to each other.

Preference for *online* also included the lack of any requirement to "dress up, waste gas, or rush about getting to church on time." Some highlighted that "there was no need to listen to or participate in the more modern music," which they referred to as "repetitive (repeating the same phrases over and over) and annoying." Many did admit that personal interaction is missing. However, in reference to church interaction, one participant articulated that "there is so much personal interaction within the church that is shallow and limited, unless you are involved with a small group where you get to know people better."

The overwhelming majority of respondents agree that the in-person church and the online church had a different overall feel to them. All seemed to value the sense of community that church services create, whether in-person or online.

CHURCH SERVICE PARTICIPATION

Those who had not yet returned to in-person services were asked how they were participating as part of the Church. They could select from the following options: Zoom, YouTube, Facebook, small group meetings with family, small group meetings with friends, none of the above, or other, and could select more than one option.

Table 12

Participation Methods: Congregants Not Yet Returned to In-Person Church

Other Activities	Number of Respondents
Zoom	41
YouTube	29
Facebook	12
Small Group Meetings with Family	1
Small Group Meetings with Friends	7
None of the Above	23
Other (e.g., personal faith, praying at home, N/A)	1*

* 1 for each option

Table 12 shows the responses, with Zoom, followed by YouTube, as the preferred method for church attendance.

These findings are interesting. The top platforms used were the same as when the closure first occurred. However, a unique outcome is that 23% of survey participants responded with the answer, "none of the above." Did 23% of them stop attending church altogether? What does that mean for the post-COVID-19 Church?

Studies show that church attendance has declined significantly in the past two years. For instance, in America, the percentage of people who attend church regularly dropped by 6%, from 34% to 28% (Wang, 2022). This is most unfortunate as Church attendance holds great significance in the believer's walk. Meeting with other believers is something we are taught to do so we can support and encourage each other. We see this Biblical example set by the early believers in the New Testament church.

REFLECTIONS

Chapter Six:
The Post-Pandemic Church

CONGREGANTS' PREFERRED METHOD OF CHURCH POST-COVID-19

During the lockdown, online was our only means to meet for church service, but with church buildings back open, we are left with an option: will we attend in-person or online? Congregants were asked to disclose their preferred format for attending church when the government declares the pandemic has ended. The response options were, "in-person," "online," or a "combination of both, if available." The following table summarizes the responses:

Table 13

Preferred Format of Church Attendance Post-Pandemic

In-Person	Combination of Both	Online
64%	6%	30%

As you can see, nearly ⅔ of the respondents favored in-person services, with close to ⅓ choosing to participate online, and a small percentage preferring the combination of both.

Key reasons for in-person preference included the command in scripture to "assemble" (Heb. 10:25), the tangible benefits of face-to-face interactions (peaceful aura to the heart, joy of seeing faces, sense of belonging, showing love), relationship building (being with friends and family), interaction with church family and faith community, fellowship, communal singing, receiving the eucharist, and satisfaction (feeling blessed, grateful for the opportunity to attend church).

Online reasoning was comprised of flexibility (better able to balance family/work/church), distance (can attend from any location), transportation (eliminates the need for commuting), convenience, safety (concerns about contracting the virus), less physical challenges (eliminates physical barriers, such as going up the stairs), medical condition limits (still able to participate), and weather (able to attend in inclement weather).

A combination of in-person and online services offers choices and flexibility. Reasons from the in-person and online categories are also applicable. Those who chose this combination enjoy the in-person experience, but like the option to participate online when they are sick, travelling, or there are other contributing factors making the virtual service more convenient.

Moving Forward: To Change or Remain the Same

After examining the effects of the pandemic on church activity, we encouraged congregants to look ahead at what it means for the future of the Church. Participants were asked to share their preference for the Church moving forward. They were encouraged to select whether they believed the Church should make changes or remain the same, and then give a reason for their choice. Table 14 demonstrates their responses.

Table 14

Congregants' Views: The Church to Make Changes or Remain the Same

Make Changes	Remain the Same	*Other
45%	39%	16%

*Participants did not respond directly to the question

This result was fairly close between the number of people who thought changes were necessary and those who wanted the church to remain the same. This puts church pastors, leaders, and board members in a difficult predicament as they consider the right way to move forward for their congregation.

Predominant reasons cited for *making changes* included:

"Making changes as God requires"

"Returning with precautions"

"Desire for full re-opening"

"A desire to see the church 'take up its rightful place and speak up, and speak out more on our God-given authority'"

And

"Romans 13:7 (… render therefore to all their due: taxes to whom taxes are due, customs to whom customs, fear to whom fear, honor to whom honor) has been misconstrued by pastors to remain silent"

That final reason given for change called out pastors, challenging them to speak up boldly and not be silent about issues the world is encountering.

Some of the grounds given for wanting to remain the same included:

"Continue the same with proper precautions and guidelines to prevent outbreaks from the virus"

"Online and in-person service currently exist"

"A liking for one's church"

"Not wanting to see the church impose physical distancing and mask-wearing"

"We don't need to evolve, but there are always ways we can improve"

This is a question that many in Church leadership will need to consider moving forward. The world is not the same as it was pre-COVID-19. Everyone's life has been affected in one way or another. How does the Church respond to that? How do leaders address the division caused by the pandemic? How do they cater to the group of congregants who enjoy and prefer online services?

These are all questions that pastors and other church leaders will need to face as the church re-opens and returns to some sense of normalcy.

Changes Arising from the COVID-19 Pandemic

It is no secret that the pandemic brought about great change within the Church. The findings obtained from the interview and questionnaire confirmed this. The format in which people gathered, worshipped, gave, and participated in activities all evolved during this time when the church doors were closed. The Church stepped up and adapted as necessary to stay afloat throughout the pandemic. Let's take a look at what these specific changes meant for the Church.

Technology

The most obvious shift during the pandemic was the move from in-person to online (virtual) service. In contrast to the church body gathering in a building, services were facilitated through various online mediums such as Zoom, Facebook, Twitter, Google Meet, and Livestream. This meant that someone on the church staff with technological skills needed to set up a service format for the congregants of the church to be able to access with ease.

Along with the services, other common elements of church service were forced to move online as well, such as the giving of tithes and offerings. This was of significant importance to the well-being of the Church since, as previously stated, the congregants' giving is the main source of revenue for the Church. Churches that did not already have an electronic giving platform in place were hard-pressed to set one up in a timely manner and notify the congregation of the ways available for them to give.

Administering Communion

It is one thing to stream services online and give funds electronically, but the more challenging pieces to figure out were the hands-on activities. A fundamental practice within the Church body that needed to change in the format during COVID-19 was the administering of holy communion, also referred to as the eucharist. Communion is a Christian sacrament, where believers eat bread, and drink wine (or grape juice), while remembering Jesus' sacrifice on the cross and the Covenant made. It is a holy time of remembrance which Jesus instructed his followers to partake in during the Last Supper in Matthew (26:26-28). Throughout the pandemic lockdown, congregants prepared their own emblems and administered holy communion individually while attending service online. The significance of holy communion was highlighted by Di Mauro (2020), who emphasized that "the church exists… and the sacraments are rightly administered… the correct administration of holy communion is not a matter of adiaphora—because if we don't celebrate it properly, we are, at best, a club and not a church" (p. 25).

New Volunteer Roles

Other important changes presented themselves as well: some positive, some negative, and some neutral. Volunteer opportunities were one area that grew with the pandemic. The shift to online services created new roles within the church body that we hadn't seen a need for previously, such as PowerPoint director, Livestream host, Camera operator, and more. It also required volunteers to step up into service roles, community outreach positions, and communication coordination positions. While the specifics of these roles looked quite a bit different than traditional service opportunities, the need for volunteers during COVID-19 was significant. Many of these roles that emerged out of necessity will continue, even with in-person service back in session.

Lackadaisical Attitudes

One of the negative effects we noticed among some congregants was a cavalier attitude, as they used the pandemic as an excuse for non-participation in church services or volunteer activities. It became easy to sit on the sidelines and simply "watch" church. This group within the church body will need to be addressed by pastors moving forward or the church could lose them altogether. Being involved in an area of ministry within the church helps individuals feel more connected as active members of the church family. When we become disengaged, we tend to drift away.

Pastoral Communication Across Denominations

Among pastors and leaders in the Church, we noticed a positive change in communication between congregations. There was an uptick in the level of conversations between different pastors across the city as they collaborated to try to figure out how to proceed in light of the pandemic. Pastors were put in an impossible position without a clear roadmap, so being able to converse with others in the same situation to discuss struggles with, pray with, and brainstorm ideas was crucial during this time. This gave them the opportunity to grow and learn from each other. Hopefully, they will continue regular communication with one another moving forward.

MEAL SHARING

One of the more minor changes that occurred was the elimination of some fellowship activities, for example, congregational meals. Where it was commonplace prior to COVID-19 for churches to gather together for food and fellowship, this activity ceased during the pandemic as meals prepared in others' kitchens could present a high risk of spreading germs. Any food items shared during this time were required to be store-bought and individually wrapped. This ensured freshness and cleanliness.

Changes presented themselves, but the Church remained pliable, and was able to handle the challenges with grace. Church leaders took action to ensure that the body could still partake in primary functions of worship, community, teaching, tithing, and communion with one another. Even with the format of church service shifting dramatically, God remained the same and so did the purpose of His Church.

REOPENING PLANS

All the leaders I spoke to indicated that they had a reopening plan in place for their church. Having a proposed plan assisted in alleviating some of the major concerns of those who were anxious about returning to in-person church. It also gave hope to those chomping at the bit to return to church. Findings revealed that the leaders were thorough in developing their plans.

One of the more formal plans included return dates and identified initial activities that would be executed on those dates. This included specific precautions such as: name and information intake for contact-tracing purposes, provisions for temperature checks, seating arrangements, order and length of services, and creating a team to execute the plan.

Another formal plan was developed and executed by the elders in the congregation. This plan contained responsibilities of the elders, which involved screening congregants, implementing physically-distanced seating, dispensing masks and hand sanitizer as congregants entered the building (everyone "got their dash of hand sanitizer," as the leader quipped), and placing collection plates at points of entry, to avoid passing between hands.

Other leaders designated teams of people to prepare in-depth plans that contained the same details as the above, plus additional steps, such as obtaining the expertise of frontline healthcare workers and recruiting ushers to guide congregants to their seats. One leader developed a plan and, along with the board of elders, worked through the decision-making process of the plan, which was then executed by the church's regular ministry leaders.

Churches looking for reopening advice, or hoping to bolster their plan already in place, can find sound guidance in the comprehensive handbook, *Guide to Reopening Church Services: A Step-by-Step, Biblically-Based and Research-Based Approach to Resuming In-Person Ministries*, by the Humanitarian Disaster Institute (Annan et al., 2020).

Concerns About Returning

While the results conveyed that the majority (70%) of congregants had no concerns about returning to in-person church, there are still 30% of respondents who indicated that they were concerned about returning. This means that leaders will have to consider strategies to ensure the return of this group, as some of them may continue to justify not returning to in-person church because of the pandemic. Churches may need to implement extra precautionary measures to help ease this demographic's concerns about the virus. They should not only be focused on getting them back into the church building, but also on maintaining a meaningful connection with these members in the meantime. If they feel disconnected or unseen as part of the church body, they may decide not to return at all.

Chapter Seven:
The Future of the Church

Now that the church buildings have reopened, how do the effects of COVID-19 alter the path of the church moving forward? Based on the effects of the COVID-19 pandemic, it is important to consider what the future holds for the Church. Some leaders expressed their concerns in this area, uncertain of what it means moving forward. Wright, Jr. (2020) notes that "now, however, as the months wear on, deep theological reflection is needed for considering what the pandemic means in the context of Christian faith and practice" (p. 578). This observation aligns with these leaders' concerns. For example, there is an intrinsic need for leaders to surrender to God and seek His wisdom in order to better understand world events such as this pandemic. Recognizing that God is sovereign and this pandemic did not come as a surprise to Him, should reassure leaders that He has a plan for the Church moving forward.

ADDRESSING ISSUES WITHIN THE CHURCH

One area that leaders may not be eager to deal with, is that, just as Apostle Paul boldly addressed false teachings and un-Christ-like behaviours and attitudes in the early Church, leaders will need to step up and do the same in regard to these types of behaviours among their congregation. Negative characteristics such as divisiveness, anger, rash judgment, complaining, rudeness, impatience, defiance, selfishness, and more, were exhibited by some congregants. Leaders will also need to address the issue of idleness and passiveness among some members who got a little too comfortable distancing themselves: Christians who used the pandemic as a reason to not be as committed or involved in the Church as they should.

CONTINUING COVID-19 PROCEDURES

I discovered, during my conversation with the leaders, that they believe their church will continue to do the majority of the things that it did during the lockdown. It will continue outreach programs to serve communities, it will call people to "check in with them," stay socially distanced in buildings, and wear masks, at least for the initial period upon return to in-person church. While all of these are beneficial to keeping the church population safe and showing compassion to individuals within the body, it does place a lot of responsibility on the shoulders of pastors and other leaders.

During COVID-19, leaders have been working around the clock to find solutions to problems they had never experienced before. They had to scramble to find volunteers to fit the various needs that occurred. They needed to recruit people for sanitation teams, welcome teams supplying masks and sanitizer, camera crews, livestream hosts, and more. At the same time that their need grew, churches began losing some of their usual volunteers, out of concern about COVID-19 or unwillingness to return to church. Trying to bear the weight of the additional responsibilities brought on by

COVID-19, while maintaining the normal in-person requirements, has leaders and volunteers stretched thin. This could lead to their eventual burnout, if more congregants do not step up.

LIVE STREAMING: CREATING AN INTERNATIONAL CONGREGATION

While the logistics of live streaming require a lot from the staff and volunteers, most churches see the added benefit of continuing to operate with a combination of in-person and online services. The predominant reason cited for utilizing both formats was the ability to reach or minister to another group of people who would not be able to attend in-person services for various reasons, such as being in a long-term care facility or living too far away. It would also reach congregants that may not return immediately or return at all for health or other reasons. Finally, churches would like the ability to continue to minister to church members nationally or internationally, who desire to continue being a part of an online congregation as they are now. This is a unique opportunity that presented itself to the Church through COVID-19 and the drastic increase of church streams.

One leader shared that his church increased its international audience by partnering with another body in the United States. He noted that there has been an increased desire from other pastors, internationally, for their churches to become a part of his church's global community. The result, as the pastor expressed, "will be part of our mandate as a church to fulfill its mission to not just be a local assembly but to be a great local assembly that sends people out into all the world."

Though the majority of churches plan to continue live streaming their services, not all leaders are keen on this idea. A leader who indicated a preference for in-person church believed that live streaming could be used for certain occasions, but not perpetually. He expressed his preference for in-person by explaining how he grew up without using a computer, but instead had a typewriter. He further expressed that sitting in front of a screen for too long did not make him happy. In fact, "it's not my cup of tea," he expressed. For this leader, he emphasized that "the in-person kind of worship, which involves people singing and hearing each other, is much more vital than just virtual, any day."

While pastors may have varying personal opinions about holding church services online versus in-person, they need to consider the needs and desires of their congregation. While most congregants (64%) indicated a preference for in-person church, there is still a minority (30%) that have opted for online church, and another group (6%) that would like a combination of both.

The challenge for leaders then, is finding a way to deliver services to those who will attend online. Research reveals the Church is likely to remain "both an in-person and online reality even after COVID-19," "not only because there are distinct advantages to both, but because today's children and young adults have always lived in-person and online" (Cressman, 2021, p. 46). Since COVID-19, churchgoers have become accustomed to having options for participating in church. Since the reopening of church buildings, many make a decision whether they want to attend in-person or online, based on how they are feeling that day. If they are sick, too tired, or not feeling social, they can stay home and watch church in pajamas from the comfort of their home.

While the majority of the congregation members interviewed would not consider this ideal compared to the in-person experience, is it better than the alternative of people staying home and not participating in (or viewing) church at all? Most of us would agree that it is! This is a contributing factor to the desire of many churches to maintain their online presence. It offers a unique opportunity for spiritual growth at times when people may not otherwise engage in it. Instead of congregants missing church altogether those days, they still get a version of it.

With various reasons contributing to the decision, the need for remaining online is clear for many congregations. How then can Church leaders best cater to their online audience, while maintaining and caring for their in-person flock? One option for achieving this is to offer a shorter time duration of the services, in order to maintain the interest of the online audience. We are already seeing this happen, as "preachers are including more visuals and learning to preach shorter, pithier sermons—about which few listeners complain" (Cressman, 2021, p. 48).

Leaders could also ask congregants to get dressed and turn on their cameras, to encourage direct engagement instead of a passive experience. Additionally, the Church could keep its online population involved by offering more online programs and activities. It is important that those participating online feel just as much connected and part of the Church body as those attending in-person. This can be a difficult feat to achieve, especially without meeting face to face or having any physical contact.

Church leaders can help attain this by regularly communicating with this demographic, encouraging activity in the livestream chats, and setting up virtual small groups or community groups where these members can get to know each other on a personal level.

Distance makes connection difficult, but not impossible. Keeping the members of the Church body who exist outside of the church walls consistently connected to those within, is a challenge that the church has not faced before, but it is one that can widen the reach of the Church throughout the community and the world.

The Family of God

The effect of COVID-19 was prevalent in society, but there were some changes and consequences that were unique to the Church. The impact of the pandemic was magnified due to the authorized closure by the government, a course of action that was never enacted during other pandemics in our lifetime. For this reason, *The Christian Century* (2020) stated: "While the closing of public worship and church-based outreach doesn't mean separation from God, there is real grief around the suspension of these tangible forms of connection to Christ, to others, and to the world" (p. 7).

Of course, the Church is not a corporate entity like other organizations; it is unique in the fact that it's the "ἐκκλησία" (Greek word for "Church"). The Church is a "called-out" body of believers that were engrafted into God's family through expressed faith in the Lord Jesus Christ. "Called-out" is best explained by the Scripture "*Behold what manner of love the Father has bestowed on us, that we should be called children of God...*" (1 John 3:1). When we place our faith in Jesus Christ, He welcomes us into His family as His beloved children. To further explain what it means to be engrafted into the Church, I will illustrate through this passage of Scripture:

"Then Peter said to them, "Repent, and let every one of you be baptized in the name of Jesus Christ for the remission of sins; and you shall receive the gift of the Holy Spirit. For the promise is to you and to your children, and to all who are afar off, as many as the Lord our God will call."

Acts 2:38-39

The Lord Jesus Christ established the Church and engrafted people into the church as recorded "...And the Lord added to the church daily those who were being saved" (Acts 2:47). Therefore, the unique identity of the Church guarantees its success despite challenges.

Two other strong sentiments that stood out in my research were that virtual (online) churches will be a reality of the future and that, out of the people (i.e., those on the 'fringe') who were not well connected before the pandemic, some will likely not return to the church. Therefore, it will be necessary for the Church to undertake significant rebuilding to reach this group of congregants. Another conclusion of my study on the subject is that the pandemic represented the birth, or the rebirth, of the modern Church. The Church will "rise to the occasion," for the Church triumphant is alive and well, more than ever before.

REFLECTIONS

Chapter Eight:
COVID-19 Reflections

LEADER INSIGHTS

As I concluded the interview, the final question that I asked church leaders was: "Is there anything else that you would like to share with me about your experience with the COVID-19 pandemic and your church, or the Church in general?"

Many expressed the desire to see the conclusion of the pandemic, which I think we can all relate to. Others pointed out that the pandemic brought to light some of the injustices, such as racism and inequality, that are prevalent in society. One leader expressed the notion that the devil had used the pandemic to instill fear and hopelessness in people. Some expressed that the pandemic amplified their desire to create change in meaningful ways - one stated that this was one of his greatest desires. Leaders also acknowledged that there were some good decisions made under pressure, such as using Zoom for communication and Sunday services. Another unexpected outcome of the pandemic mentioned was the demonstration of new talents that individuals developed. One of the leaders was complimented on having "a very nice radio voice," which he was told enhanced the online experience of his parishioners.

The pandemic also brought about the realization that the Church has an opportunity to help people understand that pandemics may come and go, but there is help from the Lord. As long as we are able to support each other and cooperate, we can make the Church better, even during a pandemic. Leaders admired the way people in their congregation came together and grew closer during the time physically apart. They firmly believe that Jesus is to credit for the relational growth within their churches.

The Unbreakable Church

A pandemic is simply no match for the Church. My research revealed that the Church responded effectively during COVID-19, meeting the needs of congregants and non-congregants. It represented a source of physical, mental, and emotional strength for congregants and the community alike. Though the Church was closed by order of government during this pandemic, unlike previous ones in which the Church remained open, the positive response of the Church was comparable to historical responses. Throughout history, and during COVID-19, the Church remained a beacon of light, demonstrating selfless behaviours in the community.

I believe the strength and tenacity of the Church are best encapsulated in this refrain:

Let the Church be the Church, Let the People rejoice.
Oh, we've settled the question,
We've made our choice.
Let the anthems ring out, Songs of victory swell
For the Church triumphant is alive and well. (Gaither, 1973)

Consequently, with great assurance, it is appropriate to conclude that as it was throughout previous pandemics, the Church will always remain relevant in society. This relevance will not be diminished, not by a pandemic and not by government order. God's people will find a way to worship with one another, to commune together, and to show love to the community, no matter the circumstances at hand.

REFLECTIONS

Chapter Nine:
Unshaken Faith

The events of this world can lead us to feel defeated and discouraged. For many, COVID-19 instilled great fear and confusion. Individuals encountered feelings of loneliness, anger, and hopelessness. The effects of the pandemic are not to be overlooked. 6.7 million deaths, as of January 2023, are no small matter. Some people lost loved ones due to the virus and with that, their lives will never be the same. Others developed severe anxiety or depression that was brought on by long periods of isolation. When we are hurting or scared, it can cause us to question God's goodness. We might find ourselves asking "where was God when _____ (whatever scenario happened)?"

I am no stranger to hard times or the testing of faith. I experienced depression after not fully understanding the obstacles that I would face both in my personal and professional life. Ending an 8-year relationship with a man I was planning to marry was one of the most difficult decisions I have ever made. While I knew in my heart it was the right decision, it didn't lessen the sense of loss or the emotional pain. Some years later, the loss of my great-grand-aunt, who played a pivotal role in my upbringing, left me feeling vulnerable. Experiences of racism, nepotism, and other unfair judgments caused me great distress too. I began sensing a deep unexplainable void within me that caused me to question the purpose of living. I soon became overwhelmed with emotional distress and almost lost the will to live. During moments like these, I questioned God's presence, but God saw my genuine pain and showed me that life could be lived purposefully through faith in Him. As I read in the Scriptures, *"If any of you lacks wisdom, let him ask of God, who gives to all liberally and without reproach, and it will be given to him. But let him ask in faith..."* (James 1:5-6)

At a significant turning point in my life, when I was struggling, God brought to my heart a specific reference in the Bible: Psalm 25. This chapter has been meaningful to me since that moment. Perhaps something in it will speak to you as well:

To You, O Lord, I lift up my soul.
O my God, I trust in You;
Let me not be ashamed;
Let not my enemies triumph over me.
Indeed, let no one who waits on You be ashamed;
Let those be ashamed who deal treacherously without cause.
Show me Your ways, O Lord;
Teach me Your paths.
Lead me in Your truth and teach me,
For You are the God of my salvation;
On You I wait all the day.
Remember, O Lord, Your tender mercies and Your loving kindnesses,
For they are from of old.
Do not remember the sins of my youth, nor my transgressions;
According to Your mercy remember me,
For Your goodness' sake, O Lord.

Good and upright is the Lord;
Therefore He teaches sinners in the way.
The humble He guides in justice,
And the humble He teaches His way.
All the paths of the Lord are mercy and truth,
To such as keep His covenant and His testimonies.
For Your name's sake, O Lord,
Pardon my iniquity, for it is great.
Who is the man that fears the Lord?
Him shall He teach in the way He chooses.
He himself shall dwell in prosperity,
And his descendants shall inherit the earth.
The secret of the Lord is with those who fear Him,
And He will show them His covenant.
My eyes are ever toward the Lord,
For He shall pluck my feet out of the net.
Turn Yourself to me and have mercy on me,
For I am desolate and afflicted.
The troubles of my heart have enlarged;
Bring me out of my distresses!
Look on my affliction and my pain,
And forgive all my sins.
Consider my enemies, for they are many;
And they hate me with cruel hatred.
Keep my soul, and deliver me;
Let me not be ashamed, for I put my trust in You.
Let integrity and uprightness preserve me,
For I wait for You.
Redeem Israel, O God,
Out of all their troubles! (Psalm 25)

Our faith in Jesus does not exempt us from experiencing difficulties, but it gives us the strength to get through them knowing that "I can do all things through Christ who strengthens me," borrowing from Apostle Paul in Philippians 4:13.

As difficult and scary as these past couple years have been for all of us, for me personally, the pandemic reinforced my faith in God. I turned to His word, in the Bible, as a source of comfort during this time. I brought my questions and fears to Him. The fact that Scriptures allude to phenomenons like this, helped me to realize, on multiple occasions, that nothing is out of God's control. *"And there will be great earthquakes in various places, and famines and pestilences..."* (Luke 21:11); and *"other ills." "...And power was given to them over a fourth of the earth, to kill with sword, with hunger, with death, and by the beasts of the earth"* (Rev. 6:8). As I dug into Scripture, I began to worry less, becoming more aware that pandemics are inevitable. I took the necessary precautions to try to stay safe and surrendered to God the rest that was beyond my control.

In life, we are bound to run into troubles. We will experience feelings of grief, disappointment, and heartache. Unfortunately, it is part of being human in this sinful world. We need to set our sights on Jesus because pursuing the things of this world will only leave us empty. God gives us this encouragement to cling to, saying, **"These things I have spoken to you, that in Me you may have peace. In the world you will have tribulation; but be of good cheer, I have overcome the world"** (John 16:33). This is the truth I cling to in difficult times. God has overcome this world and the final victory is His. I can have peace in Him that outweighs my troubles. It is a peace that is beyond earthly reason or circumstance - one that comes only from knowing Jesus, as illustrated by this Scripture, **"Be anxious for nothing, but in everything by prayer and supplication,** *with thanksgiving, let your requests be known to God; and the peace of God which surpasses all understanding, will guard your hearts and minds through Christ Jesus"* (Philippians 4:6-7).

REFLECTIONS

Chapter Ten:
What Does it Mean for Me?

You might be wondering, "What does this mean for me moving forward?" You may have endured difficult times over the last couple of years, or perhaps throughout your life, wrestling with who God is and where He is in all of this. I can tell you; He has never left your side. He is right there waiting, calling out to you, to return and seek refuge in Him.

The COVID-19 crisis was not the first pandemic and will likely not be the last. Seeing the world face this difficult time should light a fire within us. Though none of us knows the exact time that Christ will return, we have confidence that He will return, and this hope should have a visible impact on the way that we live our lives. We should not become nonchalant when it comes to sharing the good news of Jesus. Our days are numbered, and the call to witness is more pertinent now than ever.

EXAMINE YOUR LIFE

Is your faith being lived out on a daily basis or have you simply been going through the motions? The isolation that COVID-19 forced has made it easy for many to retreat from their relationships with others and to become complacent with their outreach efforts.

Are you seeking God daily and leaning into his purpose for your life, or have you become so comfortable chasing your own ambitions that you have drowned out the voice of God?

"Examine yourselves as to whether you are in the faith. Test yourselves. Do you not know yourselves, that Jesus Christ is in you?—unless indeed you are disqualified."

2 Corinthians 13:5

Do not Resist the Call of God

When God puts a call on our hearts, it is not always convenient with the timing and goals we have planned for ourselves. Sometimes, it requires sacrificial obedience and uncomfortable periods of growth. I have experienced multiple times in my life where I have reacted similarly to Jonah in the Old Testament... running in the opposite direction and pleading with God not to send me to "Nineveh." When you are in tune with the voice of God in your life, there is no denying it. You can try running from Him, but you will not experience spiritual peace in your life, until you lean in and fully embrace His call for you.

Seek Spiritual Mentorship

It's important to have strong spiritual examples in your life to learn from. We need people who can build us up and encourage us in our walk of faith. These should be individuals we trust to be honest with us and to offer godly Biblical wisdom. For me, my great grand-aunt was a pillar of spiritual strength when I was growing up.

She was a faithful follower of Jesus, who shaped my understanding of Him at a young age. I will forever be thankful for her influence on my Christian walk. Since her passing, in my adult life, my spiritual mentorship has come from my pastors, professors, and fellow believers within the Church: people I interact with whom I trust to provide sound Biblical insight. This is an essential part of our walk with Christ, communicating with other Christians, challenging, and encouraging one another in spiritual growth.

> *"As iron sharpens iron, So a man sharpens the countenance of his friend."*
>
> *Proverbs 27:17*

Hold Steadfast Convictions

The COVID-19 pandemic has no doubt challenged many Christians as they searched for answers to a phenomenon that they had never experienced before. But as Christians, the Holy Spirit has empowered us to deal with the challenges of life and has equipped us to remain true to our convictions that we will not despair when faced with calamities of any kind and criticisms that could cause us to doubt. Through our convictions, we must set a standard by "holding fast the faithful word as he has been taught, that he may be able, by sound doctrine, both to exhort and convict those who contradict" (Titus 1:9). Not only are Christians dealing with a pandemic that has no doubt given rise to some Christians wanting to know where is God in all of this, they are also faced with societal norms that are moving farther and farther away from Biblical truths.

It is more important now than ever, that we remain bold in our convictions and do not waver on matters of Biblical truth. When we waver, the Bible describes us as "I know your works, that you are neither cold nor hot. I could wish you were cold or hot. So then, because you are lukewarm, and neither cold nor hot, I will vomit you out of My mouth" (Revelation 3:15-16).

So, let's be followers who are "hot" or "on fire": 100% steadfast and unmoveable. Where do you reside on the thermostat?

CONTINUE MEETING TOGETHER

While attending Church is not what will get you into Heaven, the importance of meeting with other believers is stressed in the Bible on multiple instances. Sometimes, we can make excuses for why we shouldn't attend church. We often let personal preferences of worship style or preaching methods get in the way. Some of us no longer attend because we have been burned in the past by leaders or other members of the congregation. We may see Christians as hypocritical and are afraid of being hurt again. Unfortunately, this scenario happens a lot in churches. The Church is made up of imperfect people, who are bound to make mistakes and let us down. This can cause us to think that we don't need others and attempt to pursue our faith - walk completely on our own. It's easier this way, because we don't take the risk of getting hurt that comes with trusting others. While having a personal relationship with Jesus is essential, it was not God's intention for us to walk the path alone.

God created us to live in community with one another, building each other up. This is even more crucial now, with the decline of Christianity and church attendance, and the prevalence of sin in our society. We often find ourselves asking questions and seeking Biblical guidance, which is where having a spiritually sound community of believers to converse with is beneficial.

"And let us consider one another in order to stir up love and good works, not forsaking the assembling of ourselves together, as is the manner of some, but exhorting one another, and so much the more as you see the Day approaching."

Hebrews 10:24-25

God's word mentions the importance of gathering together. This verse talks about how we should not give that up, as some have done, and urges us to use it as a time to strongly encourage one another - especially as the end draws near.

CONTINUE PRAYING

The role of prayer cannot be underestimated. As believers, our ability to directly communicate with the Creator of the Universe is a gift that should not be taken lightly. When we sincerely approach God, He listens to us and His power is at work within us.

Crises have a way of bringing people to their knees, as they search for answers, comfort, and hope. My research revealed that, and not surprisingly because we see this trend with other catastrophes, the onset of the coronavirus pandemic prompted people "to pray more frequently and more fervently" (Kay, 2021, p. 26). In fact, according to the Pew Research Center, some 55% of adults reported in the spring of 2020 that they had already prayed the pandemic would end. This figure included "73 per cent of Christians and 86 per cent of people who ordinarily prayed daily." What is more, even the "less religious became somewhat more religious; 15 per cent of people who seldom or never prayed and 24 per cent of those without religious affiliation also prayed for an end to the pandemic" (p. 26).

The prayer that many people embraced during the pandemic was the prayer that Jesus taught his disciples found in Matthew 6:9-13 and Luke 11:1- 4, which is commonly known as The Lord's Prayer. To this united front of prayer, Willimon (2021) noted that "The Lord's Prayer moves us from our quiet understandable pre-occupation with this deadly virus to a surprising acclamation of the rule of Christ" (p. 40).

We are instructed in 1 Thessalonians 5, to "pray continually" (v.17). This means seeking conversation with God regularly as we go throughout our days, whether good times or bad. Often, we can become busy and caught up in our own lives, so much so that we forget to take time to commune with the Lord — as if anything could be more important. Though our prayers are not always answered the way that we hope or expect, we can trust that God is fulfilling His perfect will. The more that we lean into Him, the more our spirit will be at ease, even through times of uncertainty.

HOPE IN HEAVEN

Above all, never lose hope. When all in the world feels dark and discouraging, keep sight of the promise of Heaven that comes from placing our trust in Jesus. No matter how many hardships we face in this life, we can rest assured of how things will end.

Nothing in our lives is out of God's hands or comes as a surprise to Him. COVID-19 or any other pandemic, war, or tribulation to come cannot get in the way of His plan. Heaven is waiting for us. Heaven is waiting for you. All you need to do is place your trust in Jesus and hold steadfast to Him until your last day. He will carry you through the troubles of this world and into an eternity filled with a peace unimaginable.

> *"Therefore we do not lose heart. Even though our outward man is perishing, yet the inward man is being renewed day by day. For our light affliction, which is but for a moment, is working for us a far more exceeding and eternal weight of glory, while we do not look at the things which are seen, but at the things which are not seen. For the things which are seen are temporary, but the things which are not seen are eternal."*

> *2 Corinthians 4:16-18*

If you get nothing else out of this book, remember this: no matter the circumstance, **there is always hope: the everlasting hope in Jesus Christ.**

REFLECTIONS

References

Annan, K., Aten, J., & Louissaint, N. (2020). Guide to reopening church services: A step-by-step, Biblically-Based approach to resuming in-person ministries. Wheaton, IL: Humanitarian Disaster Institute.

Barnes, P. (2020). Plagues throughout History and Some Christian Responses. *The Reformed Theological Review, 79(2)*, 77–96.

Bible Study Tools. (2022). *Pestilence.* Retrieved on October 22, 2022, from https://www.biblestudytools.com/dictionary/pestilence/

Cressman, L. S. K. (2021). B.C. and A.C: Preaching and Worship Before COVID and After COVID. *Journal for Preachers, 44(2)*, 46–52.

Di Mauro, D. R. (2020). The Church in an Age of Pandemic — Holy Communion during Covid-19. *Lutheran Forum, 54(2)*, 25–30.

Emergency Management and Civil Protection Act, R.S.O. 1990, c. E.9. https://www.ontario.ca/laws/statute/90e09

Fagunwa, O. E. (2020). African Pentecostalism and the 1918 influenza pandemic: The supernatural amid the fearful and implications for the COVID-19 pandemic. *Christian Journal for Global Health, 7(5)*, 52–64. https://doi.org/10.15566/cjgh.v7i5.455

Fortin, J. P. (2021). Christian Discipleship as Compassionate Listening: Learning to Be Human in Times of a Pandemic. *Touchstone, 39(1)*, 28–39.

Gaither, B. & G. (1980). The Old Rugged Cross Made the Difference. Retrieved from https://www.lyricsondemand.com/g/gaithervocalbandlyrics/theoldruggedcrossmadethe-differencelyrics.html

Gaither, B. & G. (1973). The Church Triumphant. Retrieved from https://divinehymns.com/lyrics/let-the-church-be-the-church-song-lyrics/

Gillen, A. L. (2009, October 25). Biblical Leprosy: Shedding Light on the Disease that Shuns. *Answers Magazine.* Retrieved from https://answersingenesis.org/biology/disease/biblical-leprosy-shedding-light-on-the-disease-that-shuns

González, C. G. (2020). Christians' Responses to Plagues: A Glimpse at the History. *Journal for Preachers, 44(1)*, 15–21.

Greene WC 2007. *A history of AIDS: Looking back to see ahead.* Eur J Immunol 37 Suppl. 1: S94–S102.

History.com Editors (2021, December 2021). Pandemics That Changed History. Retrieved March 15, 2022, from https://www.history.com/topics/middle-ages/pandemics-timeline

History.com Editors (2020, May 19). Spanish Flu. Retrieved March 15, 2022, from https://www.history.com/topics/world-war-i/1918-flu-pandemic

History.com Editors (2021, February 21). History of Aids. Retrieved March 15, 2022, from https://www.history.com/topics/1980s/history-of-aids

Just, B. (2020, April). Historic plagues and Christian responses: lessons for the church today? *Christian Journal for Global Health, 7(1),* 7-12.

Kay, J. F. (2021). The Paradox of Prayer in a Time of Pandemic. *Journal for Preachers, 44(4),* 26–33.

Merriam-Webster. (n.d.). Pandemic. In *Merriam-Webster.com dictionary.* Retrieved October 22, 2022, from https://www.merriam-webster.com/dictionary/pandemic

Molina, A. (2020). Larger Churches urged to Help Smaller Ones Survive Pandemic. *The Christian Century, 137(10),* 17–18.

Pew R.C. Social and Demographic Trends. 2020. 2020b. *Most Americans Say Coonavinus Outbreak Has Impacted Their Lives.* [Google Scholar! March 30 [Ref list]

Rae, R. & Zeng, A. (2006, February 7). SARS in Canada. *The Canadian Encyclopedia.* Retrieved from https://www.thecanadianencyclopedia.ca/en/article/sars-severe-acute-respiratory-syndrome

The Christian Century (Eds.). (April 8, 2020). Being the church without being together. *The Christian Century, 137*(8), 7.

The Holy Bible: KJV, NKJV, NLT.

The Province of Ontario, Office of the Premier (2020, December 21). *Ontario Announces Provincewide Shutdown to Stop Spread of COVID-19 and Save Lives.* [News Release]. Retrieved from https://news.ontario.ca/en/release/59790/ontario-announces-province wide-shutdown-to-stop-spread-of-covid-19-and-save-lives

Wang, W. (2022, January 20). The decline in church attendance in Covid America. *Institute for Family Studies.* Retrieved October 27, 2022, from https://ifstudies.org/blog/the-de-cline-in-church-attendance-in-covid-america#:~:text=A%20new%20IFS%20analysis%20using,2019%20to%2028%25%20in%202021.

Willimon, W. H. (2021). Praying the Lord's Prayer in a Pandemic. *Journal for Preachers, 44*(4), 34–41.

World Health Organization (COVID-19). Retrieved from https://covid19.who.int

World History Encyclopedia (n.d.). *Plague of Cyprian 250-270 CE*. Retrieved October 22, 2022, from https://www.worldhistory.org/article/992/plague-of-cyprian-250-270-ce/

Wright, A. M., Jr. (2020). God and the Pandemic: A Christian Reflection on the Coronavirus and its Aftermath. *Review & Expositor, 117*(4), 578–579.

Appendix A

Description of Denominations

Denomination	Description
Anglican	Base their Christian faith on the Bible, traditions of the apostolic Church, apostolic succession and the writings of the Church Fathers ("Anglicanism", 2021)
Baptist	Forms a major branch of Protestant Christianity distinguished by baptizing professing Christian believers only (i.e., adults), and doing so by complete immersion ("Baptists", 2021)
Free Methodist	A denomination of Methodism, which is a branch of Protestantism. It is believed that the name, Free Methodist, comes from their belief that it was improper to charge for better seats in pews closer to the pulpit, their opposition to slavery and their support for freedom for all slaves in the United States ("Free Methodist Church in Canada", 2021).

Pentecostal	Emphasizes the direct personal experience of God through baptism with the Holy Spirit. The term Pentecostal is derived from Pentecost, an event that commemorates the descent of the Holy Spirit upon the followers of Jesus Christ, and the speaking in "foreign" tongues as described in the second chapter of the Acts of the Apostles ("Pentecostalism", 2021).
Presbyterian	Emphasizes the sovereignty of God, the authority of the Scriptures, and the necessity of grace through faith in Christ. Its roots originated in the Reformation of the 16th century, the example of John Calvin's Republic of Geneva being particularly influential ("Presbyterianism", 2021).
Roman Catholic	Bases its core beliefs on the Nicene Creed. It teaches that it is the one, the holy, catholic, and apostolic church founded by Jesus Christ in his Great Commission, that its bishops are the successors of Christ's apostles, and the pope is the successor to Saint Peter, upon whom primacy was conferred by Jesus Christ ("Catholic Church", 2021).
Seventh-day Adventist	Distinguished by its observance of Saturday, the seventh Adventist day of the week in Christian and Jewish calendars, as the Sabbath and its emphasis is on the imminent Second Coming (advent) of Jesus Christ ("Seventh-day Adventist", 2021).

About the Author

Claudette E. Miller
D. Min (IP), M. Div., M. Ed., B. ADED, B.A., CHRM

Reverend Claudette E. Miller is a doctoral student at Canada Christian College & School of Graduate Theological Studies, located in Whitby, Ontario, Canada. On June 4, 2022, she graduated from this institution with a Master of Divinity and was Valedictorian of the graduating class.

Following a successful career in public sector management, Claudette is transitioning from corporate life to Christian ministry to fulfill the call of God in her life to share the Gospel of Jesus Christ.

While pursuing studies at Canada Christian College & School of Graduate Theological Studies, Claudette preached on various occasions, which afforded her the opportunity to demonstrate the call to ministry. One of her favourite Bible characters is Apostle Paul who was given the formidable task of preaching the "Message of Grace" far and wide. It is only fitting that one of her first messages was "God's Amazing Grace." She loves to tell of God's abundant grace, through her own experience and that of others in the Bible.

In addition to a Master of Divinity, Claudette holds a Master of Education, a Bachelor of Adult Education, a Bachelor of Art, a Certificate in Human Resources Management, a Certificate in Adult Education & Staff Training, and a Diploma in Theology. Throughout her career, Claudette studied part-time, during which she achieved most of her academic accomplishments. She also made time to volunteer in the church, in the community, and in her workplace.

Claudette believes strongly in education and has worked tirelessly from a very young age to achieve an excellent academic standing. This is a value that her mom instilled in her and her siblings early on in life. She is incredibly passionate about both her salvation and her education. She desires to see all young women and men fulfill their dreams and aspirations in life through the Lord Jesus Christ. Claudette acknowledges that her faith in Jesus Christ gave her strength, making it possible to succeed during times when the odds were against her. There were many times throughout her educational endeavors when roadblocks would have made it easy to give up, but her faith in Jesus gave her the courage to continue on. Thus, her motto became: Salvation + Education = Success!

Based on Claudette's childhood, especially her formative years in the New Testament Church of God in Jamaica, it is not a surprise to see that, years later, she is embarking on this new journey in response to the direct calling of God. As a child, she was active in the church: singing, reciting, acting, and fundraising. She was affectionately called "The Little Evangelist" by her spiritual leaders. Scriptures declare *"train up a child in the way he should go: And when he is old, he will not depart from it"* (Prov. 22:6). Claudette is a keen example of this verse lived out. Though her faith went through periods of weakness as a young adult, the foundational knowledge of Biblical teachings always rang true in the back of her mind. She is thankful to have experienced the love of Jesus at such a young age.

Claudette was brought up in the church as a child, but drifted away as a young adult as she pursued her education, her career, and her own desires, not giving much thought to her relationship with Jesus or the truth she had learned when she was younger. It was at 28 years old that Claudette felt God tugging on her heart, and saying, "Return to me." As resistant as she felt initially, Claudette could not deny the overwhelming presence of God and surrendered her life entirely to him. She has been pursuing Him passionately since that day.

She is forever grateful to those God placed in her life at that time, who spurred her on in her walk with Him and helped reassure her of his call in her life.

Reverend Claudette understands the importance of responding to the voice of God in your life, even when it seems inconvenient. She is committed to pursuing His will for her, in this new chapter, as she heads into full-time ministry.

In the recent TED talk titled "Destiny: Navigating between Career and Calling," Claudette painted a vivid picture of a pivotal, awe-inspiring moment. This moment signaled that a transition to a new career was due to fulfill her purpose. Consequently, this realization led to the creation of her book, "Faith Amid the COVID-19 Crisis" — available at https://www.positionedforpurpose.com/about-me or search for "Claudette Miller TEDx" on YouTube.

If you're ready to step onto the path of self-discovery, visit www.positionedforpurpose.com. There you'll find services to help you discover your resilience, rekindle your faith even when hope may seem elusive, and find empowering tools to help you embrace your destiny. Don't just exist, thrive in your purpose. The tools for your journey await.

For inquiries email: millercl@positionedforpurpose.com

Made in the USA
Monee, IL
09 August 2023

40613891R00075